Pedagogy
Using Television Shows, Games, and Other Media in the Classroom

Edited by
Laura Dumin
University of Central Oklahoma

Series in Education

⬛ VERNON PRESS

www.vernonpress.com

In the Americas:	*In the rest of the world:*
Vernon Press	Vernon Press
1000 N West Street, Suite 1200	C/Sancti Espiritu 17,
Wilmington, Delaware, 19801	Malaga, 29006
United States	Spain

Series in Education

Library of Congress Control Number: 2024932858

ISBN: 979-8-8819-0167-7

Also available: 978-1-64889-901-0 [Hardback]; 979-8-8819-0027-4 [PDF, E-Book]

Cover design by Vernon Press. Background image by Freepik.

Table of Contents

List of Figures

List of Tables

Introduction

Laura Dumin

University of Central Oklahoma

As technology shifts, so should our teaching methods. Sometimes, though, instructors struggle to see how or where they can make changes that move beyond the trendy. Allowing students to make TikToks? Ok, but why? Having students perform songs about Shakespeare? Cool, but how does that demonstrate topic knowledge? Building a website to show ancient indigenous cooking methods? Neat idea, but have students clearly linked this back to the historical concepts of the curriculum content? These questions are just the tip of the iceberg for figuring out how to embrace new technologies while still making sure that students take away some sort of topic knowledge.

Varying our teaching styles and content presentation can keep the content interesting to a wide variety of learners. While the idea of learning styles has been mostly debunked (Willingham et al, 2015), students can still benefit from moving beyond the traditional written presentation of material (Carter, 2021; Lawless, n.d.). This book will look at various classroom types, starting with primary and secondary education spaces, moving to the writing classroom in higher education, and then moving beyond the writing classroom. Authors present a variety of educational projects that seek to engage learners and help students to more deeply learn and retain the curriculum information.

Book Chapter Overview

The first section of the book looks at teaching in primary and secondary education classrooms. How can we engage students in exciting and meaningful ways to enhance their learning?

Trudeau gives us an example of using VR headsets to bring experiential learning into the classroom in a cost-effective and manageable way. While we can't take our students on all the field trips and we can't go to all the historical sites, with VR technology, we can bring those sites to the students. In so doing, we help our students to better understand history and cultural situations in ways that create deeper connections than just reading or watching videos can.

Simmons looks at teaching hard concepts such as human rights through a boardgame. Trying to teach younger students about heavy concepts can be challenging because of their emotional development and because of parental concerns. Games can take some of the pressure off teachers to teach all the nuances while giving students a chance to genuinely participate in their own learning.

Wythe takes on the engagement of students with autism spectrum disorder (ASD), looking at gamification strategies to help students want to participate in the learning. Two studies are presented here to show different strategies for employing gamification to knowledge for students.

Wickham looks at middle school student writing projects and how adding a multi-genre approach to teaching can help students build better projects, noting that "the best teachers cannot rely on static curricula because they know that students' needs, interests, and motivations change, just as the world around us evolves" (p. 51, this volume). She also looks at some of the impacts of artificial intelligence (AI) on our classrooms and our students.

The next section of the book focuses on higher education and writing classrooms. Canfield discusses the use of podcasts and student reactions to the assignment. She also gives an answer to the question "Are podcasts academic writing?" Incorporating podcasts into her teaching allows students to have the opportunity to learn about audience and presentation as well as word-choice, making this an engaging way to teach students about what can count as academic writing.

Schuermann focuses on games and how they can be used in the higher education classroom. This chapter presents a themed first-year composition course based on digital game design and development that utilizes digital games' affordances through four major writing assignments based on digital game composition writing and collaborative writing, concluding with suggestions for instructors interested in engaging students in creative ways and in developing their own writing courses based on digital game design and development.

Dumin focuses on using podcasts, TV shows, and articles to teach about intersectionality and DEI topics. Students had the opportunity to explore the American Dream and what college education can do for social mobility, while also exploring their own identities and how they fit into their communities. Student responses to the project and the use of podcasts are included here, as well as a discussion about how podcasts impacted this particular classroom.

The last section of the book looks at classrooms outside of the writing classroom, thinking about ways to creatively engage students in the content.

Atwood introduces us to the use of video games and movie music to help students relate to Medieval music and the history of the music. Noting that little has survived from the original music, and students may not have heard much of the music outside of popular culture depictions, this can be a way to bring students back to the lessons and actively engage in learning the material.

Copley discusses the use of clear gamification goals to motivate students to learn more deeply, noting also that poor gamification strategies stress students out and can lead to negative learning goals. She gives the example of using Classcraft.com, a free resource, to help increase students' learning and retention of information.

Conclusion

The purpose of this book is to highlight creative and innovative teaching methods that can more deeply engage students across educational contexts. The chapters provide examples of using technology, games, multimedia projects, and other novel approaches to make content more relatable, participatory, and memorable for learners. While adhering to curriculum standards and learning objectives remains important, these chapters illustrate the value of varying instructional formats to promote enthusiasm for learning.

A key takeaway is that there are many untapped opportunities for experimenting with new platforms and assignments while still ensuring academic rigor. For instance, several chapters discuss how multimedia projects enable students to demonstrate comprehension of topics in alternative ways, apply concepts practically, collaborate with peers, and gain technical abilities—all highly relevant skills. Finding the right balance is critical; poorly implemented gamification risks trivializing content rather than making it stick. Hence following established best practices around goal-setting, scaffolding complex tasks, providing actionable feedback, and linking novel activities directly to core academic concepts is vital.

Much work remains in systematically evaluating the impacts of creative teaching methods on indicators like knowledge retention over time, critical thinking abilities, metacognitive skills, and perceptions of learning. Nonetheless, the preliminary evidence and examples shared here make a compelling case for diversifying instructional strategies beyond traditional lectures and writing assignments. The authors have provided springboards for teachers to adapt existing ideas or brainstorm new innovations tailored to their subjects, students, and institutions. With some risk-taking and refinement over time, such approaches may meaningfully catalyze student motivation and comprehension.

References

Carter, A. (2021). *Exploring the benefits of blended and multimodal learning.* https://www.astoncarter.com/en/insights/articles/exploring-the-benefits-of-blended-and-multimodal-learning

Lawless, C. (n.d.) *Multimodal learning: Engaging your learner's senses.* LearnUpon Blog. https://www.learnupon.com/blog/multimodal-learning/

Willingham, D. T., Hughes, E. M., & Dobolyi, D. G. (2015, July 15). The scientific status of learning styles theories. *Teaching of Psychology, 42*(3). https://doi.org/10.1177/0098628315589505

K-12 Classrooms

Chapter 1

Virtual Reality: A Pathway to Experiential Learning

Andrea Trudeau

Northern Illinois University

Abstract: Trudeau gives us an example of using VR headsets to bring experiential learning into the classroom in a cost-effective and manageable way. While we can't take our students on all the field trips and we can't go to all the historical sites, with VR technology, we can bring those sites to the students. In so doing, we help our students to better understand history and cultural situations in ways that create deeper connections than just reading or watching videos can.

Keywords: VR headsets; experiential learning; history; culture

***

Introduction

Credited with founding the field of virtual reality (VR), Jaron Lanier asserted, "'Virtual' means something that exists only as an electronic representation . . . It's as if it were there even if it isn't" (Heilbrun, 1989, p. 110). By harnessing the power of VR, educators of today have the ability to transport students to times and places that would otherwise be inaccessible to them in a traditional classroom setting, providing them with opportunities to witness key moments in history firsthand, work on the International Space Station, or even travel through the bloodstream to learn how blood cells function. Immersive VR provides students with captivating learning experiences where they may visit the world all around them or worlds within themselves—places they may never see otherwise due to numerous factors, including cost, conflicts in time or schedule, or potential risks (Alhalabi, 2016). Through the power of VR, what was formerly inconceivable now becomes possible without ever leaving the confines of the classroom.

Virtual reality is just one of several forms of instructional technology that is increasingly being harnessed in smart learning environments (SLEs) found in classrooms today. "Smart learning refers to learning in interactive, intelligent, and personalized environments with the support of cutting-edge digital technologies and services" (Chen et al., 2021, p. 2). Gwak (2010) suggested smart learning prioritizes learners and content over devices while advocating for intelligent, effective, personalized learning facilitated by an advanced technological infrastructure. In a smart learning environment, teachers harness adaptive, innovative technology, such as VR, to engage a variety of learners. Through VR, students experience a virtual environment that mimics reality through 360-degree images or videos and stereoscopic sound, which promotes the interactive, adaptive, and personalized learning experience expected in an SLE.

Currently, VR is expected to have a compound annual growth rate of 37.9% in the global education market (The Business Research Company, 2023) and is most frequently being applied through science- and engineering-related subject areas, especially at the secondary level (Luo et al., 2021; Tilhou et al., 2020; Zhang & Wang, 2021). In these settings, students are provided with hands-on opportunities to both construct and deconstruct models and prototypes, practice using various technologies related to particular fields and run simulations. Consequently, VR has been shown to improve student engagement, provide opportunities for simulated real-world experiences without ever leaving the confines of the classroom, and enhance students' short-term and long-term retention of information.

As educators today strive not just to reinforce students' academic skills but also to foster their overall well-being, VR may be harnessed as a vehicle to support students' social-emotional learning (SEL) and promote global consciousness through immersive and interactive cinematic virtual reality (CVR) films. In CVR films, viewers are enveloped in a 360-degree experience with the story taking place all around them. This grants them the power of an omnidirectional view. In other words, they are no longer confined to the traditional rectangular view prescribed by the film director; instead, they can determine where they wish to direct their gaze as the story progresses around them, even interacting with the story in some instances. Consequently, CVR provides students with a means to experience "a story that you would remember with your entire body and not just with your mind" (de la Peña, 2015, 00:06). Whether a student is engaging in a hands-on VR activity or consuming a CVR film, they have a powerfully visceral experience that can have a profound impact on them both in the short-term and long-term.

The Power of Immersion

Many highly immersive VR systems of today are composed of a head-mounted display (HMD) and handheld controllers. HMDs come in many forms—some that require the user to hold the device to their face, while others include head straps, which allow the user to wear the device and, consequently, frees up their hands to hold paired handheld controllers for a more interactive experience. The HMD has a built-in computer that presents two images to the user's eyes, which, in turn, creates an illusion of depth. Sensors within the headset work with the user's movements to alter scenes and generate a new reality within this headset. When a user looks in various directions, the visuals respond accordingly where real-world perceptions are replaced with those digitally generated. Immersion in a VR world is generated through visual cues, sounds, and other stimuli much like what one would experience in the real world (Bucher, 2018; Freina & Ott, 2015); in turn, immersion leads to a sense of presence—or the feeling of being in a new reality (Alhalabi, 2016; Bailenson, 2018; Bambury, 2019; Chen et al., 2019; Wu et al., 2021). In short, immersion refers to the level of a sensory experience generated by the VR equipment while presence is the psychological response the user has as a result. As immersion increases, presence also increases, which results in users experiencing a deeper emotional response (Bambury, 2019; Calvert & Abadia, 2020; Chen et al., 2019; Durnell, 2018; Schott & Marshall, 2018; Wu et al., 2021). Increased presence in a VR world also fosters transformational learning experiences for individuals (Calvert & Abadia, 2020; Chen et al., 2019; Kwon, 2018; Wu et al., 2021).

The Application of Virtual Reality in the Classroom

Virtual reality can be used in a variety of ways in K-12 classrooms, especially as an increasing number of educational VR applications are being developed for student use:

- **Virtual Field Trips**—Through pre-created tours, teachers gain the ability to transport their students to places that they may never see otherwise—museums, sites of cultural and/or historical significance, and places of interest around the world. Some examples of this include Nearpod VR, ClassVR, Unimersiv, SchooVR, and Expeditions Pro.
- **Immersive Learning**—VR can be utilized to immerse students into learning environments that allow them to see the world like never before and in unimaginable ways—inside the human body or exploring the natural habitat of animal species. Some examples of this include The Body VR, VR Anatomy, Google Earth VR, Ocean Rift, and Titans of Space.
- **Simulation Learning**—Simulations in VR provide students with hands-on learning experiences in a real-life scenario that allow them to use the tools of the trade, harness their critical thinking skills, and apply methods for problem-solving. Some examples of

this include Job Simulator, Flight Simulator VR, Fantastic Contraption, and Roomle.

- **Language Learning**—Through VR, students are presented with a virtual environment that simulates real-world situations. Students then may practice their language skills by interacting with artificial intelligence-driven characters in a range of scenarios. Some examples of this include Mondly, ImmerseMe, and NounTown.

- **Interactive Storytelling**—In an interactive storytelling experience, students gain the ability to participate in a story and their choices determine the outcome—much like a modern-day *Choose Your Own Adventure*. Some examples of this include Moss, Wolves in the Walls, and The Great C.

- **Remote Learning**—Through VR, learning in a classroom is merely a headset away. VR classrooms allow individuals to come together in a virtual learning space to interact with each other and learn together. Some examples include ENGAGE, Virbela, Mozilla Hubs, and Second Life.

Virtual reality has the potential to revolutionize modern-day classroom instruction by providing immersive and interactive learning experiences that engage students and enhance their knowledge of complex concepts and skills through real-time feedback. Ultimately, this improves the accessibility of students' learning experiences through a personalized approach that not only addresses their individual needs but also addresses their unique interests.

Constructivism

The immersive and interactive experiences VR technology provides are harnessing the power of constructivism. A constructivist approach to learning asserts that learning is the result of individuals creating their own sense of knowledge based on their prior experiences and new events. Constructing knowledge is an active process on the part of the learner and can be influenced by social experiences and interactions with each other (Dewey, 1938; Vygotsky, 1978). A constructivist classroom is an interactive, student-centered space; lessons designed with the theory of constructivism in mind are "active, effective, and meaningful, and result in superior learning" when compared to those that are more traditional, teacher-led, and passive (Fegely et al., 2020, p. 522).

At the heart of constructivist learning is an experience—a novel experience that blends with a student's previous experience to create new meanings. It is an active process that is dependent on sensory input to construct meaning. Virtual reality provides this digital experience and through immersion and interactivity, engages the user's senses to promote learning. In Laverick et al.'s manuscript (2020), the researchers asserted that VR could provide powerful experiential learning experiences to build students' background knowledge and promote comprehension skills—especially when an authentic real-world experience is not possible. They connected their study to the work of John Dewey's Experiential Learning Theory (1938), which asserts the value of learning through the context of an experience. Traditional learning was composed of classroom instruction, which typically included lectures and reading, so learning occurred through the absorption of knowledge conveyed by another. Dewey's theory provides a more active learning approach, where students learn through doing (1938), which later leads to constructivism. Laverick et al. (2020) noted that by utilizing VR in the classroom, secondary students participate in an independent discovery process where they can connect with content more deeply and build a knowledge base through personal experiences, which remains with them and supports them as they encounter new content in the future to support deeper levels of reading comprehension.

Experiential Learning

Digitally generated VR worlds provide a powerful pathway to Kolb's Experiential Learning Cycle (2015) where "knowledge results from the combination of grasping and transforming, and transforming experience is how individuals interpret and act on that information" (p. 51). The Experiential Learning Cycle, as illustrated in Figure 1.1, operates as a spiral, where the learner must go through the four stages and may do so many times—"experiencing, reflecting, thinking, and acting" to learn, unlearn, and relearn (Kolb, 2015, p. 51). This type of learning should occur in an authentic context and center around realistic, open-ended learning experiences, which provide opportunities for students to utilize the tools of trade. Through these types of experiences, students engage in real-world learning through active participation, problem identification, information gathering, and decision-making.

Figure 1.1. The Four Stages of Kolb's Experiential Learning Cycle

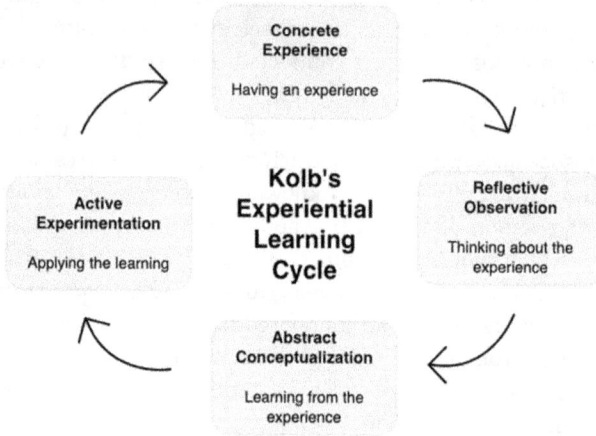

When students place the VR HMDs on their heads and pick up the coordinating hand controllers, they can learn by doing and progressing through Kolb's (1984; 2015) four stages outlined in the Experiential Learning Cycle. Since learners have diverse backgrounds and different schemata, not only does Kolb's Experiential Learning Cycle support students' individual needs, but it also offers more engaging and active learning experiences (Kolb, 1984, 2015; Konak et al., 2014). The immersive nature of VR has the power to open incredible doorways for learners to experience different worlds and different perspectives that provide them with relevant, meaningful hands-on learning opportunities. Consequently, a powerful transaction occurs between a learner and the environment where experience becomes the bedrock for learning (Kolb, 2015). Research demonstrates students who participate in experiential learning opportunities demonstrate increased levels of excitement about school, higher levels of motivation, a stronger connection to lessons and activities, and enhanced learning outcomes (Konak et al., 2014; Schott & Marshall, 2018; Scogin et al., 2017). In Villena-Taranilla et al.'s (2022) recent meta-analysis of the application of VR in elementary school settings, it was concluded that immersive VR utilized in short intervals led to the greatest impact on students' learning gains—and even more so than experiences students had in semi- or non-immersive VR worlds for a longer period. However, it is important to note that the notion of "experience" in Kolb's 1984 Experiential Learning Theory was based on an in-person experience with physical interactions in a setting. Over 35 years later, educators can utilize VR as a vehicle for providing their students diverse, meaningful experiential learning opportunities that allow them to work through the four stages of Kolb's Experiential Learning Cycle without ever having to leave the classroom.

This was demonstrated in Schott and Marshall's (2018) study where university students visited the Fiji Islands to learn more about life on the island as well as sustainable practices. After visiting this virtual world, participants noted a strong sensory response to the experience. One-third of respondents in the study noted they tried to reach out and touch objects due to the immersive nature of the experience and others even shared that their bodies had a physical reaction to the experience, "[T]here was a weird tingly sensation in my knees and my legs as I was walking through the grass because it felt like there should be something there" (Schott & Marshall, 2018, p. 848). This experience, which respondents repeatedly called "real" helped them get a stronger sense of the culture of the Fiji Islands and provided them with opportunities to learn in ways that wouldn't necessarily be possible in a physical world—through curated experiences, translators, and an insider's view to the issues at hand. In turn, this made complex concepts more readily accessible to them and resulted in a much deeper understanding of the issues the Fiji Islands faced. Virtual reality provided them with a doorway to Fijian life they may not otherwise experience.

This notion of "experience" in the Experiential Learning Cycle carries a double meaning and relates not just to the actions but also to the emotion of the experience (Kolb, 2015). Durnell's (2018) dissertation research examined the power of experience within a virtual reality headset and the resulting residual emotional impact. Adult participants viewed and interacted with the United Nations-sponsored film, *Clouds Over Sidra*, co-created by Chris Milk and Gabo Aroba, which follows the story of a 12-year-old refugee girl named Sidra. After the film, subjects noted that "the immersive experience can offer a place to begin necessary conversations and confirmed how these conversations can be used to share information on a person-to-person level" (Durnell, 2018, p. 100). Durnell examined tweets from subjects post-viewing and determined that respondents demonstrated a strong understanding of the refugee crisis due to the emotional experience VR provided them, and, as a result, were compelled to act. Applying Kolb's Experiential Learning Theory in a virtual reality setting supports individuals' deeper understanding of concepts while also improving their motivation and attitudes about a topic for memorable, long-lasting effects.

By combining virtual reality and the Experiential Learning Cycle, not only does the learner have a deeper learning experience, but it also impacts the learning outcomes. Alhalabi's 2016 study demonstrated that students learning new content using a highly immersive head-mounted virtual reality display system had, on average, quiz scores that were 25% higher than those who took the quiz after receiving information without VR and in a more traditional learning setting. Tenth-grade students who participated in Chen et al.'s study (2019) and learned how to build a quadcopter using virtual reality demonstrated a stronger knowledge of complex scientific concepts as well as improved hands-on abilities when compared to peers who worked without VR. Through VR, they were able to employ Active Experimentation and run the simulation tests of their quadcopter, which supported their problem-solving skills and developed their knowledge. Konak et al. (2014) determined in their research study with first- and second-year college students studying information security that those who followed the Experiential Learning Cycle-aligned framework demonstrated a deeper understanding of complex concepts, showed more interest, and had higher perceived competence. Through the application of experiential learning, students were able to contextualize learning experiences through hands-on activities; when these activities also included collaborating with their peers, students achieved a higher level of understanding of the subject matter, indicating the value of collaboration in the learning cycle.

Virtual Reality Systems in Education

Just as VR technology has experienced significant advances in recent years, the headsets have evolved as well. This is reflected in the wide range of VR equipment currently in use in K-12 classrooms. When determining an approach for VR implementation in the classroom, it is important to consider the following: the learning goals for harnessing this technology, the age and skill level of the students, the technology infrastructure available in the learning space, technical support and training, management of the devices, safety and comfort, long-term viability, and, of course, both time and cost.

The use of VR in the classroom has been a gradual process with many educators taking the initial leap into VR in 2014 with Google Cardboard. Just as its name indicates, Google Cardboard is a budget-friendly option made of cardboard that, when folded properly, transforms into a VR headset with a flap that opens in the front for the user to secure a smartphone inside. The smartphone, which requires the installation of VR applications, becomes the operating system for the VR experience. Other companies, such as Merge and Samsung, have released their own versions, crafted of sturdy foam or plastic material, which offer more hygienic options for sharing among students since they can be easily wiped down between uses to ensure cleanliness. Some of these headsets require the user to hold the headset to their face, while others include straps to free up a user's hands. Referred to as a smartphone VR headset or mobile VR headset, this approach to VR equipment allows educators to use this experiential technology tool with students easily and with minimal cost to schools; it does require the acquisition of smartphones, which can come from a variety of sources, including donations or students' personal devices. When students are asked to utilize their personal devices, permission should be obtained from students' caregivers for the installation of VR apps. All apps, regardless of whether a student installs it, or the installation is done by school staff, should be carefully vetted for age appropriateness. Lastly, if the budget allows, schools may wish to look into RedboxVR, which are kits that include both headsets and unlocked Google Pixel devices, which allow for the installation of a wide range of compatible software for classroom use.

Another type of VR equipment utilized in schools today is tethered VR headsets, such as HTC Vive, Oculus Rift, PlayStation VR, and Windows Mixed Reality. (See Figure 1.2) Instead of a smartphone, this type of headset requires a physical connection to a high-performance computer or gaming console through HDMI or USB cables, which then creates high-quality imagery and a more immersive experience. The computer or gaming console processes and renders the VR experiences while the headset operates as the interface for the user's interactions within the environment; working in conjunction with the headsets are hand controllers, which allow users to engage and interact with the environment. Tethered headsets also require external sensors, which are mounted around the perimeter of the play area through hardware or sensor stands. The sensors track both the position and movement of the user through the headset and hand controllers, resulting in responsive visuals and audio that create a more immersive, realistic experience. Due to the equipment and set-up requirements, tethered headsets are best suited for dedicated VR play spaces. This set-up may also require a second student to supervise the user wearing the VR headset since they can easily become tangled in the cables connecting the headset to the external computing device. Because this type of headset is connected to an external device, it can also be connected to an external monitor, which allows those not wearing the headset to get the same view that the user sees while experiencing the virtual space. This approach allows students to demonstrate their learning through screenshots and screen-recorded videos.

More recently, there has been a shift to wireless all-in-one VR headsets where there is no longer a need for a smartphone, and the user is freed from tethered cables; this includes headsets such as Meta Quest, ClassVR, Pico VR, and Apple Vision Pro. The necessary components—display, processing unit, and sensors—are all built directly into the headset. The headset also includes inside-out tracking technology, where the cameras and sensors are built directly into the headset to track the user's movements, eliminating the need for external sensors. Consequently, students may explore virtual worlds more safely—without the concern of getting tangled in the tethered wires. It also allows them to work more independently; they no longer need a spotter to ensure that they remain safe in the play area. While this eliminates the direct connection to the desktop computer, there are options to cast a user's view to a device to capture the user's learning experience through still images or videos. Lastly, the hand controllers allow a user to draw out the play area or select stationary play, eliminating the need for sensors within a dedicated space for VR and thus making this equipment more flexible and able to be applied more readily in various settings around a school—even shared among classrooms and educators.

Figure 1.2. Student Wearing Meta Quest 2 Head-Mounted Display

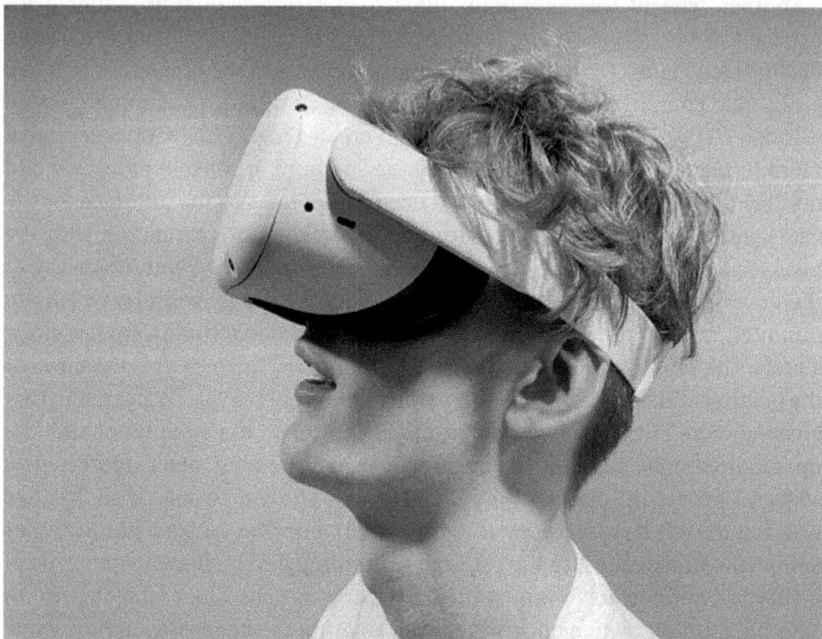

When exploring virtual reality systems, it becomes crucial to discern between commercial tools designed for general use and those specifically created for educational application in the classroom. VR headsets such as Google Cardboard and Meta Quest were created for individual users, so educators harnessing these tools will find themselves a great deal of time vetting and curating applications to determine those appropriate for student use. They also will spend an inordinate amount of time installing these apps on each individual device being utilized. Meanwhile, VR tools intended for classroom use, such as RedboxVR and ClassVR, make the experience of using VR much more time-efficient for educators while providing high-quality, standards-aligned content for learners. With these types of VR platforms, educators are provided with a management system that allows for content to be easily pushed out to an entire class set of headsets at one time, saving them both time and frustration. Students' attention may also be monitored and even directed during the actual VR experience through a teacher device. Newer versions of these devices also include handheld remotes, which provide increased interactivity and result in a more personalized experience for students.

Health and Safety Considerations

Ensuring the health and safety of students is paramount when incorporating VR into educational settings. Currently, the International Age Rating Coalition (IARC) recommends the use of commercial headsets for those 13 years old or older (Meta, 2023). It is important to note that commercial headsets were designed for adult users and, therefore, may be heavy or cumbersome for younger users. While ClassVR notes their headsets are designed for middle or high school students, their website includes case studies that showcase usage among students as young as preschool-age (Avantis Systems, Ltd., 2023).

One concern often cited about the use of VR headsets with students is eye health. Currently, there are limited studies that explore how VR affects children's eye development, and those conducted only include small sample sizes that cannot be generalized to a broader audience. However, the American Academy of Ophthalmology's official stance is VR will not pose a threat to children's eye development or overall health (Mukamel, 2017). Ophthalmologist Dr. Stephen Lipsky noted, "Age limitations for VR technology might make sense for content, but as far as we know this technology poses no threat to the eyes" (Mukamel, 2017). However, more studies must be conducted to explore the potential long-term effects on eye health and development.

When VR headsets are in use, students should be closely monitored by adults in the classroom to ensure there are not any adverse effects. Virtual reality headsets require the eyes to focus and converge at a fixed distance, which can lead to a condition called vergence-accommodation conflict (Kramida, 2016). When this happens, the eyes converge to a certain point in space while the lens inside the eye does not adjust to focus on that point as it would in the real world. This can lead to side effects for the user. Coined by Kay Stanney (1995), "cybersickness" refers to the various side effects that some users experience while using VR: headaches, blurry vision, motion sickness, disorientation, and instability. Therefore, teachers working with students in VR should ask them how they feel during the VR experience, as some students may hesitate to self-advocate. For some students, these effects will resolve themselves as they continue their VR experience while others may find the effects troublesome and need a practical alternative to VR. Some of the applications or CVR films found in VR have online alternatives that may provide a less immersive 360-degree experience, which allows students to participate in a way that is more comfortable for them. Teachers should consider limiting the amount of time students spend in a headset and may also encourage students to stay seated during the VR experience to minimize some of the effects.

Getting Started in Virtual Reality

Virtual reality is an engaging experiential technology tool that can be harnessed to complement instruction and used for pre-teaching to build background knowledge (Laverick et al., 2020) or to provide extensions to instruction, which ultimately deepens students' knowledge through active learning, critical thinking, and civic engagement (Fegely et al., 2020). When first exploring VR in the classroom, it can be overwhelming to determine how best to initiate its use. It is recommended to start by utilizing applications that promote the consumption of content. Tools such as Google Arts and Culture, YouTube VR, and RYOT have content worth exploring for classroom use and are an easy and inexpensive way to get started. As with any tools being used in the classroom, it is important to vet and preview content to ensure that it is appropriate for student viewing before use.

When examining VR content, it can become confusing because content labeled as VR does not always distinguish between two-dimensional, 360-degree still, or moving images viewed on a computer screen from immersive VR worlds experienced in HMDs with handheld remotes. Fransson et al. (2020) and Maas & Hughes (2020) argue that these should not be referred to interchangeably as virtual reality since each type of instructional technology provides a distinct experience and results in a different type of engagement among student users. Therefore, it is important to be mindful not just of the content but also of the way in which users interact with the content to ensure the appropriate technology tools are available and it is meeting the learning objectives.

Cinematic Virtual Reality (CVR)

With students becoming increasingly more likely to watch videos to learn a concept or just for pleasure, cinematic virtual reality, or CVR, is a powerful vehicle educators can harness to teach content to their students. In a CVR film, the viewer is no longer separated by the intermittent space between themselves and the screen and instead becomes a participant in the 360-degree landscape that envelopes them (Bosworth & Sarah, 2019; Constine, 2015). Bosworth and Sarah (2019) call this "breaking the fourth wall" where a viewer can make direct eye contact with characters in the film, making a much deeper connection to the characters and the story they experience in VR. In turn, research has shown users feel a stronger sense of embodiment and agency, which results in an increase in empathy among users (Barbot & Kaufman, 2020; Thériault et al., 2021).

Coined "the ultimate empathy machine" by Chris Milk in his 2015 TED Talk, CVR is gaining ground in the film industry with a growing number of filmmakers creating CVR films to raise awareness, elicit emotional responses, and inspire both short-term and long-term prosocial behaviors. Initially, CVR films were intended for adult audiences and have been studied extensively in the field of media arts. These studies have found that virtual reality evokes a strong emotional response in adults (Calvert & Abadia, 2020; Chen et al., 2019; Cohen et al., 2021; Ding et al., 2018; Durnell, 2018; Herrera et al., 2018; Rodrigues & Loureiro, 2021; Tan et al., 2022; Tian et al., 2021; Wu et al., 2021) as well as increased motivation to support causes (Fegely et al., 2020).

However, filmmakers have begun expanding their work to younger audiences with an increasing number of films rated "E" for Everyone and to support the development of "global consciousness" (Rifkin, 2010, p. 178). With a greater emphasis on educating the whole child through social-emotional learning (SEL) instruction and preparing students to be global citizens of the future, CVR films hold immense potential in providing powerful "mirrors, windows, and sliding glass doors" (Bishop, 1990) for students to validate diverse perspectives, ultimately improving the relationships students have with others and even with themselves.

For example, students studying the Civil Rights Movement may explore a stand-alone CVR film called *Traveling While Black* (Felix & Paul Studios et al., 2019) where they find themselves in the famous Ben's Chili Bowl in Washington D.C., listening to powerful stories from Black Americans, which transport them to various times within history to bear witness to the racism experienced by Blacks in the United States. The filmmaker intentionally places the viewer in settings with a unique vantage point to create a more immersive experience— such as sitting in a booth with individuals both across from them and next to them as if they are part of an intimate conversation or sitting at the back of the bus in the Black section to gain a sense of that perspective. Student viewers of this award-winning CVR film are often seen reaching out to touch things around them and speaking out loud to characters as if they are there. Conversations with students after this 20-minute experience in VR demonstrate learning about the Black experience in American history through this experiential technology has profound effects on students' comprehension and emotional responses that affect them both immediately and for weeks following their viewing.

Another powerful CVR film is the documentary *The Displaced* (Ismail & Solomon, 2015), which is available through Within (previously Vrse), an app that contains a vast array of films. *The Displaced* is rated "E" for Everyone and was created by Within filmmakers Imraan Ismail and Ben C. Solomon in 2015 in conjunction with *The New York Times*. In a mere 11 minutes, the viewer is transported to the worlds of three child refugees and is face-to-face with Oleg, an 11-year-old boy living in eastern Ukraine; Chuol, a 9-year-old boy from South Sudan; and Hana, a 12-year-old girl living in Syria. A recent study of seventh-grade students by Trudeau et al. (2023) noted that this film had a statically significant impact on adolescent students' cognitive and affective empathy scores as measured on the Adolescent Measure for Empathy and Sympathy (Vossen et al., 2015) with a more remarkable increase among male students. One male student viewing the film, who is on the autism spectrum, was observed trying to speak to Oleg at the very start of the film, reaching out and saying, "Hey there, friend." This student's cognitive and affective empathy scores doubled when his pre-test and post-test scores were analyzed.

Through CVR films such as *Traveling While Black* and *The Displaced* as well as many others available as stand-alone films or within various applications, students can experience the world through a viewpoint that may be different than their own; the immersion and interactivity students experience contributes to their sense of presence and ultimately exhibit higher levels of engagement:

- *Home After War: Returning to Fear in Fallujah* (NowHere Media, 2020)
- *How Do We Love Thee* (Gardner, 2021)
- *The Key* (Bradbury & Tricart, 2020)
- *Notes on Blindness* (Brett et al., 2016)
- *On the Morning You Wake (to the End of the World)* (Novelab, Atlas V, & Archer's Mark, 2022)
- *We Live Here* (Alfrobel Inc., 2020)

By utilizing CVR, users participate in an independent discovery process where they can connect with media more deeply and build a knowledge base through personal experiences, which remain with them and support them as they encounter new content. In turn, these encounters lead to rich post-film conversations in the classroom and result in meaningful, memorable learning experiences for students.

Moving From Consumption to Creation of Content

While exploring VR content within an HMD is a powerful experiential learning experience for students, it is vital for students to have opportunities for content creation as well. To meet the needs of today's learners, "educators must shift from a teaching-centered paradigm toward a learner-centered paradigm" and provide them with opportunities "to utilize higher-order thinking skills such as analysis, synthesis, and evaluation" (Roehl et al., 2013, p. 45). Consequently, educators can elevate their application of VR in the classroom by moving from students' mere consumption of VR content to providing meaningful and memorable learning opportunities for students to create their own content.

Platforms for Content Creation

To extend students' application of VR from consumption to creation, there are different tools available to them:

- **CoSpaces Edu**—CoSpaces Edu by Delightex (https://www.cospaces.io/) is a device-agnostic cloud-based tool that has both free and subscription-based versions—both of which provide students with a platform for creating and sharing virtual worlds. Through CoSpaces Edu, students may work solo or collaboratively to create immersive and interactive learning experiences that demonstrate their learning. (See Figure 1.3) CoSpaces EDU includes a library of content that can be dragged and dropped into a building space with the option to utilize uploaded content as well as code using CoBlocks, a scripting language similar to Scratch. It includes a VR option along with augmented reality (AR) options, including building content on a Merge Cube, which can be physically manipulated in the hands of the user to explore a student-created world. They also offer a range of tutorials and resources to help teachers get started, including video tutorials, lesson plans, and a community forum to connect with other educators and creators.

Figure 1.3. A CoSpaces Edu Project

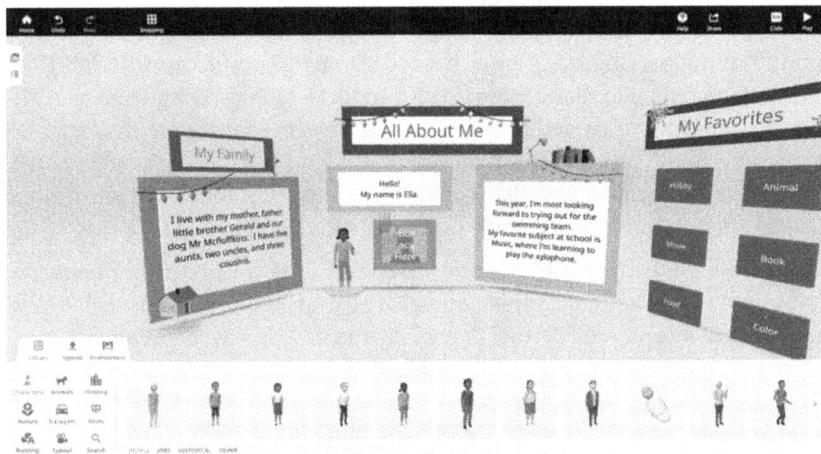

Note. From Virtual Presentation, by Delightex, 2023, CoSpaces Edu (https://edu.cospaces.io/GQB-QXM).

- **Unity 3D**—While this tool has a steeper learning curve than CoSpaces Edu, Unity 3D by Unity Technologies (https://unity.com/) is a downloadable application with free and subscription-based options that are widely utilized for the creation of VR and AR experiences. Unity provides access to advanced graphics, built-in physics, and robust animation tools while providing users with the ability to code using a range of programming languages, such as JavaScript and C#. Unity's Asset Store provides access to pre-built resources, including three-dimensional (3D) models, audio files, and plugins that expedite the creation process. Due to its wide use in building a range of applications that can be run on various platforms, Unity has active online community participation in forums where users can connect with others and access both resources and tutorials.

Tools to Support VR Creation

While VR creation platforms provide preloaded content, students may occasionally find it limiting, sparking their desire to create and upload their own content using a variety of tools. Two primary areas of interest for students in content creation are landscapes and 3D objects. For landscapes, students can create a 360-degree photosphere or a skybox. A photosphere is formed by seamlessly stitching together photographs, which serve as immersive landscapes in VR that envelope users during their experiences. On the other hand, a skybox provides students with an opportunity to experiment with digital visual elements, allowing them to fabricate stylized or fantastical landscapes. In addition, students can harness the power of photogrammetry, employing apps that collect, interpret, and measure data from photographs to build realistic-looking 3D models. Moreover, students have the creative freedom to create their own digital objects to integrate into their VR landscape. In the ever-evolving realm of VR, students can emerge as architects of immersive landscapes and 3D wonders, empowering them to craft unique virtual environments, bound only by their creativity and imagination.

To create landscapes for VR worlds, students have a variety of options. For 360-degree photospheres, a free option is PolyCam 360 Capture (https://learn. poly.cam/360-capture). This tool seamlessly stitches together panoramic images, with the added benefit of artificial intelligence (AI) filling in the uncaptured sky and ground sections. If a budget permits the acquisition of additional equipment, students can delve into the world of 360-degree photography using cameras such as Ricoh Theta or Insta360. When evaluating options like these, it is essential to weigh the cost and skill level of the students using them. Creating a 360-degree photosphere involves capturing a series of photos and then seamlessly stitching them together. While certain cameras automate this process, others may require users to perform this manually using dedicated software, which can be both time-consuming and labor-intensive for students. Lastly, students may opt to create a skybox for their VR landscape. Blender, a robust animation software tool, provides a canvas for crafting the six faces of a skybox. Students can also generate an extraordinary virtual world through Blockade Lab's tool, Skybox Lab, with just a few keystrokes.

Students may also aspire to create 3D objects to integrate into their VR worlds. However, this task is more intricate than a simple online search and upload, as this approach would yield a flattened representation within the virtual space. Consequently, students must leverage specialized tools to craft their own 3D objects. Tools such as Tinkercad, SketchUp, or Blender are robust 3D model creation tools that offer user-friendly interfaces and features to facilitate the design and construction process. Other innovative tools, such as Qlone or Polycam, employ photogrammetry, a technique that involves capturing and interpreting data from photographs taken on mobile devices, to generate lifelike 3D objects to be integrated into virtual reality worlds. (See Figure 1.4.)

Figure 1.4. Using Qlone to Scan a Shoe for a 3D Model

Conclusion

Virtual reality provides a "computer-generated digital environment that can be experienced and interacted with as if that environment were real" (Jerald, 2016, p. 9). In Chris Milk's (2015) TED Talk, he elaborated,

You feel your way inside of it. It's a machine, but inside of it, it feels like real life, it feels like truth. And you feel present in the world that you're inside and you feel present with the people that you're inside of it with.

By harnessing VR tools and applications, students have the opportunity for engaging and fun learning experiences that boost their knowledge and content-related skills as well as opportunities to develop the 5 Cs—communication, creativity, collaboration, critical thinking, and curation. Virtual reality provides a digitally created authentic learning context where Durnell (2018) asserts that "classrooms can be extended from the physical space to the virtual space in order to fulfill students' needs and to allow students to participate in a collaborative learning style" (p. 101). Students are transported to a location through the VR headset, allowing them to travel to places they may never see in real life to experience a location firsthand and have opportunities to be equipped with tools of the trade to address the ill-structured problems they face in a virtual space.

Learning in a VR environment becomes highly individualized based on the choices the learner makes. "Interactive games of this kind use a teacher-pupil model to adapt the task to the learner's needs, and a task model to provide meaningful feedback on their actions. This means interactive technologies can provide personalized help on a daily basis in a way that is difficult to achieve in a demanding classroom environment" (Frith et al, 2013, p. 9). It also allows the instructor to support students and facilitate learning but lets the student take the center seat in learning—doing so through trial and error and through making decisions and seeing the consequences of those decisions.

With the increasing availability of VR tools in schools today, it is becoming more accessible and affordable for educators to incorporate this experiential technology into their teaching practices. Virtual reality has the potential to revolutionize the way we teach, transforming the learning landscape for today's students. By immersing learners in simulated environments, learning becomes more accessible and personalized for students, which deepens students' understanding of themselves, others, and the world around them.

References

Alfrobel Inc. (Producer). (2020). *We live here* [Film]. Oculus.

Alhalabi, W. (2016). Virtual reality systems enhance students' achievements in engineering education. *Behaviour & Information Technology, 35*(11), 919-925. https://doi.org/10.1080/0144828X.2016.1212931

Avantis Systems, Ltd. (2023). *ClassVR.* https://www.classvr.com

Bailenson, J. (2018). *Experience on demand: What virtual reality is, how it works, and what it can do.* W. W. Norton & Company.

Bambury, S. (2019, December). *The depths of VR model 2.0.* VirtualiTeach. https://www.virtualiteach.com/post/the-depths-of-vr-model-v2-0

Barbot, B., & Kaufman, J. C. (2020). What makes immersive virtual reality the ultimate empathy machine? Discerning the underlying mechanisms of change. *Computers in Human Behavior, 111,* 106431. https://doi.org/10.1016/j.chb.2020.106431

Bishop, R. S. (1990). Mirrors, windows, and sliding glass doors. *Perspectives: Choosing and Using Books for the Classroom, 6*(3), ix-xi.

Bosworth, M., & Sarah, L. (2019). *Crafting stories for virtual reality.* Routledge.

Bradbury, G. (Producer), & Tricart, C. (Director). (2020). *The key* [Film]. Lucid Dreams Productions.

Brett, M. (Producer), & Colinart, A., La Burthe, A., Middleton, P., & Spinney, J. (Directors). (2016). *Notes on blindness* [Film].

Bucher, J. K. (2018). *Storytelling for virtual reality: Methods and principles for crafting immersive narratives.* Routledge, Taylor & Francis Group.

The Business Research Company. (2023). *Virtual reality in education global market report 2023.*

Calvert, J., & Abadia, R. (2020). Impact of immersing university and high school students in educational linear narratives using virtual reality technology. *Computers & Education, 159,* 104005. https://doi.org/10.1016/j.compedu.2020.104005

Chen, J., Huang, Y., Lin, K., Chang, Y., Lin, H., Lin, C., & Hsiao, H. (2019). Developing a hands-on activity using virtual reality to help students learn by doing. *Journal of Computer Assisted Learning, 36*(1), 46-60. https://doi.org/10.1111/jcal.12389

Chen, X., Zou, D., Xie, H., & Wang, F. L. (2021). Past, present, and future of smart learning: A topic-based bibliometric analysis. *International Journal of Educational Technology in Higher Education, 18*(1). https://doi.org/10.1186/s41239-020-00239-6

Cohen, D., Landau, D. H., Friedman, D., Hasler, B. S., Levit-Binnun, N., & Golland, Y. (2021). Exposure to social suffering in virtual reality boosts compassion and facial synchrony. *Computers in Human Behavior, 122,* [106781]. https://doi.org/10.1016/j.chb.2021.106781

Constine, J. (2015, February 1). *Virtual reality, the empathy machine.* TechCrunch+. https://techcrunch.com/2015/02/01/what-it-feels-like/

de la Peña, N. (2015, November). *The future of news? Virtual reality* [Lecture transcript]. TED. https://www.ted.com/talks/nonny_de_la_pena_the_future_of_news_virtual_reality

Delightex. (2023). *Virtual presentation* [Image]. CoSpaces Edu. https://edu.cospaces.io/GQB-QXM

Dewey, J. (2015). *Experience and education.* Free Press. (Original work published 1938)

Ding, N., Zhou, W., & Fung, A. Y. (2018). Emotional effect of cinematic VR compared with traditional 2D film. *Telematics and Informatics, 35*(6), 1572-1579. https://doi.org/10.1016/j.tele.2018.04.003

Durnell, L. (2018). The emotional reactions of viewing a crisis in virtual reality (VR). Fielding Graduate University. https://www.researchgate.net/publicatio

n/341679758_The_Emotional_Reactions_of_Viewing_a_Crisis_in_Virtual_R eality_VR

Fegely, A. G., Hagan, H. N., & Warriner, G. H., III. (2020). A practitioner framework for blended learning classroom inquiry-based virtual reality lessons. *E-Learning and Digital Media, 17*(6), 521-540.

Felix & Paul Studios (Producer), & Williams, R. R. (Director). (2019). *Traveling while black* [Film].

Fransson, G., Holmberg, J., & Westelius, C. (2020). The challenges of using head mounted virtual reality in K-12 schools from a teacher perspective. *Education and Information Technologies, 25*(4), 3383-3404. https://doi.org/10.1007/s10 639-020-10119-1

Freina, L., & Ott, M. (2015). *A literature review on immersive virtual reality in education: State of the art and perspectives.* https://www.itd.cnr.it/download/ eLSE%202015%20Freina%20Ott%20Paper.pdf

Frith, U., Bishop, D., Blakemore, C., Blakemore, S.-J., Butterworth, B., & Goshwami, U. (2013). Neuroscience: Implications for education and lifelong learning. *Integrating Science and Practice, 3*(1), 6-10. https://citeseerx.ist.psu.edu/view doc/download?doi=10.1.1.680.7080&rep=rep1&type=pdf

Gardner, A. [EDU CVR]. (2021, February 21). *How do we love thee* [Video]. YouTube. https://youtu.be/pr4BHInq2OI

Heilbrun, A. (1989). An interview with Jaron Lanier. *Whole Earth Review*, (Fall), 108-119.

Herrera, F., Bailenson, J., Weisz, E., Ogle, E., & Zaki, J. (2018). Building long-term empathy: A large-scale comparison of traditional and virtual reality perspective-taking. *PLOS ONE, 13*(10), e0204494. https://doi.org/10.1371/jo urnal.pone.0204494

Ismail, I., & Solomon, B. C. (2015). New York Times: The displaced. *Within.*

Jerald, J. (2016). *The VR book: Human-Centered design for virtual reality.* Association for Computing Machinery and Morgan & Claypool.

Kolb, D. A. (1984). *Experimental learning: Experience as the source of learning and development.* Prentice-Hall.

Kolb, D. A. (2015). *Experiential learning* (2nd ed.). Pearson Education.

Konak, A., Clark, T. K., & Nasereddin, M. (2014). Using Kolb's Experiential Learning Cycle to improve student learning in virtual computer laboratories. *Computers & Education, 72*, 11-22. https://doi.org/10.1016/j.compedu.2013. 10.013

Kramida, G. (2016). Resolving the vergence-accommodation conflict in head-mounted displays. *IEEE Transactions on Visualization and Computer Graphics, 22*(7), 1912-1931. https://doi.org/10.1109/TVCG.2015.2473855

Kwon, C. (2018). Verification of the possibility and effectiveness of experiential learning using HMD-based immersive VR technologies. *Virtual Reality, 23*(1), 101-118. https://doi.org/10.1007/s10055-018-0364-1

Laverick, D., Paquette, K., & Sibert, S. M. (2020). Virtual reality experiences as an instructional strategy for promoting comprehension. *Reading Improvement, 57*(4), 173-179.

Luo, H., Li, G., Feng, Q., Yang, Y., & Zuo, M. (2021). Virtual reality in K-12 and higher education: A systematic review of the literature from 2000 to 2019. *Journal of Computer Assisted Learning.* https://doi.org/10.1111/jcal.12538

Maas, M. J., & Hughes, J. M. (2020). Virtual, augmented and mixed reality in K–12 education: A review of the literature. *Technology, Pedagogy and Education, 29*(2), 231-249. https://doi.org/10.1080/1475939X.2020.1737210

Meta. (2023). *Welcome to the Oculus safety center.* Meta Quest. https://www.ocu lus.com/safety-center/

Mukamel, R. (2017, February 28). *Are virtual reality headsets safe for eyes?* (S. Lipsky, Ed.). American Academy of Ophthalmology. https://www.aao.org/eye -health/tips-prevention/are-virtual-reality-headsets-safe-eyes#:~:text=Most %20VR%20headset%20manufacturers%20say,eye%20development%2C%20 health%20or%20function

Novelab, Atlas V, & Archer's Mark (Producers). (2022). *On the morning you wake (to the end of the world)* [Film]. ARTE France.

NowHere Media (Producer). (2020). *Home after war: Returning to fear in Fallujah.* [Film].

Rifkin, J. (2010). *The empathic civilization: The race to global consciousness in a world in crisis.* Jeremy P. Tarcher, Inc.

Rodrigues, M. B., & Loureiro, S. M. C. (2021). Virtual reality in the motion picture industry: The relationship among movie coolness, sympathy, empathy, and word-of-mouth. *Journal of Promotion Management, 28*(2), 144-159. https://d oi.org/10.1080/10496491.2021.1987964

Roehl, A., Reddy, S. L., & Shannon, G. J. (2013). The flipped classroom: An opportunity to engage millennial students through active learning strategies. *Journal of Family & Consumer Sciences, 105*(2), 44-49. https://pdfs.semantics cholar.org/daa3/b94cdc7b52b3381a7c7e21022a7a8c005f84.pdf

Schott, C., & Marshall, S. (2018). Virtual reality and situated experiential education: A conceptualization and exploratory trial. *Journal of Computer Assisted Learning, 34*(6), 843-852. https://doi.org/10.1111/jcal.12293

Scogin, S. C., Kruger, C. J., Jekkals, R. E., & Steinfeldt, C. (2017). Learning by experience in a standardized testing culture. *Journal of Experiential Education, 40*(1), 39-57. http://doi.org/10.1177/1053825916685737

Stanney, K. (1995). Realizing the full potential of virtual reality: Human factors issues that could stand in the way. *Proceedings Virtual Reality Annual International Symposium '95,* 28-34. https://doi.org/10.1109/VRAIS.1995.512 476

Tan, M. C. C., Chye, S. Y. L., & Teng, K. S. M. (2022). "In the shoes of another": Immersive technology for social and emotional learning. *Education and Information Technologies, 27,* 8165-8188. https://doi.org/10.1007/s10639-022- 10938-4

Thériault, R., Olson, J. A., Krol, S. A., & Raz, A. (2021). Body swapping with a black person boosts empathy: Using virtual reality to embody another. *Quarterly Journal of Experimental Psychology, 74*(12), 2057-2074. https://doi. org/10.1177/17470218211024826

Tian, F., Hua, M., Zhang, W., Li, Y., & Yang, X. (2021). Emotional arousal in 2D versus 3D virtual reality environments. *PLOS ONE, 16*(9), e0256211. https://doi.org/10.1371/journal.pone.0256211

Tilhou, R., Taylor, V., & Crompton, H. (2020). 3D virtual reality in K-12 education: A thematic systematic review. In S. Yu, M. Ally, & A. Tsinakos (Eds.), *Emerging technologies and pedagogies in the curriculum* (pp. 169-184). Springer.

Trudeau, A., Xie, Y., Ketsman, O., & Demir, F. (2023). "Breaking the fourth wall": The effects of cinematic virtual reality film-viewing on adolescent students' empathic responses. *Computers & Education: X Reality, 2,* 100009. https://doi.org/10.1016/j.cexr.2023.100009

Villena-Taranilla, R., Tirado-Olivares, S., Cózar-Gutiérrez, R., & González-Calero, J. A. (2022). Effects of virtual reality on learning outcomes in K-6 education: A meta-analysis. *Educational Research Review, 35,* 100434. https://doi.org/10.1016/j.edurev.2022.100434

Vossen, H. G., Piotrowski, J. T., & Valkenburg, P. M. (2015). Development of the adolescent measure of empathy and sympathy (AMES). *Personality and Individual Differences, 74,* 66-71. https://doi.org/10.1016/j.paid.2014.09.040

Vygotsky, L. S., Cole, M., Stein, S., & Sekula, A. (1978). *Mind in society: The development of higher psychological processes.* Harvard University Press.

Wu, H., Cai, T., Luo, D., Liu, Y., & Zhang, Z. (2021). Immersive virtual reality news: A study of user experience and media effects. *International Journal of Human-Computer Studies, 147,* 102576. https://doi.org/10.1016/j.ijhcs.2020.102576

Zhang, W., & Wang, Z. (2021). Theory and practice of VR/AR in K-12 science education—A systematic review. *Sustainability, 13*(22), 12646. https://doi.org/10.3390/su132212646

Chapter 2

A World in Crisis! Using Games to Teach Human Rights Concepts in Elementary Classrooms

Jon Simmons

University of Connecticut

Abstract: Simmons looks at teaching hard concepts such as human rights through a boardgame. Trying to teach younger students about heavy concepts can be challenging because of their emotional development and because of parental concerns. Games can take some of the pressure off teachers to teach all the nuances while giving students a chance to genuinely participate in their own learning.

Keywords: human rights; board games; emotional development

***

Introduction

The preamble to the Universal Declaration of Human Rights states that teaching and education to promote respect for human rights and freedoms is necessary in order to guarantee global recognition and observance of human rights. Article 26, which states that everyone has the right to education, further goes on to explain that

> Education shall be directed to the full development of the human personality and to the strengthening of respect for human rights and fundamental freedoms. It shall promote understanding, tolerance and friendship among all nations, racial or religious groups, and shall further the activities of the United Nations for the maintenance of peace. (United Nations, 1948)

Since 1948 ideas about human rights education have been widely explored. The UN declared 1994-2005 the decade for Human Rights Education, and at the conclusion of the decade, it launched the World Programme for Human Rights which will continue to emphasize human rights education through 2024. Understanding the fundamental principles of human rights prepares students to fully exercise their civic responsibilities in a global context. In 2015, the National Council for Social Studies endorsed human rights education as "a necessary element of social studies programs and should be integrated throughout the educational experience of all learners from early childhood through advanced education and lifelong learning" (National Council for the Social Studies, 2015, p. 161). Even with 70 years of discussion surrounding human rights education, it remains peripheral to American education. Additionally, teachers can be hesitant to discuss human rights concepts in their classroom, citing their own lack of knowledge and training. Further, teachers often express concern that there will be pushback from parents if they discuss human rights concepts. This chapter explores ideas about education, challenges, and innovations in teaching human rights, and proposes a new strategy to introduce human rights into a classroom using games. Additionally, this chapter outlines the process of creating a game to address human rights concepts.

Human Rights Education

Human rights education (HRE) is broadly defined as learning that develops the knowledge, skills, and values of human rights. The goal is to build a universal human rights culture with students who are aware of the issues and who are concerned and capable of standing up for human rights. Human rights can only be achieved through the continuous demand of informed people for their protection. Education is essential to this idea. Approaches to HRE are generally broken into three lenses: knowledge, skills, and values. Knowledge centers on learning about human rights and promoting awareness and understanding of human rights issues. Skills can be viewed as learning for human rights. A skills focus includes critical thinking, recognition of bias, and positive conflict resolution to develop abilities necessary for the defense of human rights. The final approach, values, can be considered as learning through human rights, developing empathy, justice, and respect to end violations.

These ideas can seem like a continuum. First, we must learn what human rights are before we can learn to respect, protect, and defend them. And many curriculum programs treat them as a sequence with a suggested progression of topics. Early childhood education should begin with respect for self, parents, and community. Ages 8-11 focus on group rights, citizenship, and social responsibility. Adolescence targets specific understandings of human rights and international law. Finally, teenagers focus on moral responsibility and integration of human rights into personal behavior (United Nations Publication, 2004; Asia Pacific Human Rights Information Center, 2003). This progression mirrors theories of child development; viewing young children as egocentric and older adolescents as more able to think abstractly about the rights of others.

Human Rights Education includes a myriad of concepts and ideas. Freedom, peace, dignity, sustainability, diversity, citizenship, cooperation, social justice, empathy, respect, politics, social-emotional learning, multiculturalism, and democracy are just some of the terms associated with HRE. Some of the pedagogical terms used to describe the teaching of HRE include learner-centered, participatory, dialogical, action-oriented, flexible, relevant, and holistic integration. Looking at this list of terms can be overwhelming for an educator. And to wrap all these ideas and more into a single curriculum or lesson is a daunting task. Further, one must consider the context in which these lessons are taught. For example, the Asia Pacific Human Rights Information Center lesson plan guide (2003) includes lessons about the right to work during the dry season, an important topic in the monsoon climate region. Considering context is important to help prepare students to address human rights within both their home context and other contexts.

Many human rights curriculums include a section on pedagogy or methods. They advocate using a variety of methods to instruct HRE. The Advocates for Human Rights, an organization that strives to promote international human rights standards offers a collection of lesson plans and resources for teachers featuring a variety of different approaches. Another resource might be *The World as it Could Be*, a curriculum and resource guide for teachers (Sohcot et al., 2019). Discussion comes up frequently, as it enables students to explore issues for themselves. Cooperative learning and group projects feature in most curriculums as a space for students to practice ideas of fairness and equality through the completion of a project. Many curriculums encourage teachers to use a variety of media, including film, photography, newspaper, radio, and filmmaking to facilitate learning. Another common feature is creative expression, which can take the form of poetry and creative writing, graphic arts, song, dance, or drama. Role-playing and simulation also feature in most curriculums. These methods all revolve around the idea that HRE is more than just subject matter. Many curriculums note that teachers need to "walk the walk" and embody the underlying principles of human rights in their lives. For example, a teacher who tells the class they will be learning about freedom of expression and then in the next breath scolds a student for saying something they disagree with isn't living human rights principles. The wide range of concepts to teach and methods to use can be challenging for teachers, who may not know where to start.

Challenges and Getting Started

As discussed in the previous section, HRE includes a wide range of topics and approaches, which leave teachers feeling unsure of how to integrate human rights content into their classrooms. Imagine for a moment that you are an elementary school teacher who is interested in human rights. You do some research online to see how to begin. As you look through different lessons and curriculums and see the long list of different ideas that are associated with human rights education, you begin to feel very overwhelmed. You find online manuals, some of which are hundreds of pages long! You begin to question how you could fit any of these lessons into your day when you are already behind, and the pressure of the looming state standardized test is mounting. You wonder how to connect these lessons to your standards and content, as many of these links are not clearly articulated. You might be feeling intimidated at the prospect of discussing racism, genocide, torture, and other controversial topics in your class. How will the students respond? Is this even appropriate to talk about with elementary students? What will your administration say? What will the parents say?

These are all concerns that teachers might face as they begin to think about how to add HRE to their elementary school classrooms. On top of that, you may or may not have had any training about how to teach human rights concepts. Another challenge teachers must navigate is how much of their own values to share in the classroom. Current ideas about teaching often suggest that teachers should suppress their own individual political and religious ideas. This is difficult to do. Students pick up on the values of their teachers and may subconsciously seek to mirror those values. Students may not feel empowered to disagree with their teachers. Further, teachers must decide if they present these issues as settled or ongoing. When presenting ideas as settled students are not invited to explore the idea and develop new learning, as they get to do when human rights issues are presented as ongoing. In a classroom discussion on Nazi propaganda, one student brought up the idea that the holocaust had been just. In that moment, the teacher had to decide if she would allow the class to explore this idea and develop their own idea, or if she should shut it down (Bickmore, 2014). These types of professional judgments are daunting for teachers and often serve as barriers to teaching about human rights. Further, teachers who wish to emphasize the agency of young students and position them as agents of change may seek opportunities for young learners to simultaneously learn what human rights are and how to protect them. Here is the challenge of HRE: how does one present human rights ideas in a way that excites learners and motivates them to take an active role in the promotion and protection of human rights?

Innovative Approaches

There are some creative and innovative approaches to teaching human rights such as Write 4 Rights, the global letter-writing campaign run by Amnesty International (2018). Write 4 Rights highlights profiles of people across the globe who have had their rights taken away and asks participants from across the globe to band together to write letters of support and demand change. Classrooms can participate, connecting this to their language arts curriculum, as most grade levels do some form of persuasive writing. Another innovative approach would be to connect the tenets of service learning to HRE (Padilla, 2011).

Other organizations have similar ways to engage students in their HRE work. Justseeds Artists' Cooperative features projects with a human rights twist. One project uses the articles of the Universal Declaration of Human Rights as inspiration for linocut prints. Another project uses multiple media to create artwork centered on the importance of clean drinking water. Justseeds produced a book, *Firebrands*, which features mini-biographies of social justice luminaries from across North, Central, and South America. ARTE, which stands for Art and Resistance Through Education, uses art to start dialogues about social justice and human rights issues amongst youths. StoryCorps strives to share stories capturing the gamut of human experiences to foster compassion in the world. The tradition of theater of the oppressed encourages people to take active roles in political simulations. They use the theater as a way for people to take on different roles, try different solutions, and have a dialogue about social issues. Educators can borrow from any of these innovative approaches to human rights education.

Games in Schools

Could there be a role for games in the landscape of HRE? When one plays a game, they temporarily suspend reality to enter the world of the game. In the world of the game, there are different rules and expectations. This offers an interesting potential to think about games as a place where some of the challenging conversations teachers were worried about having may be more easily approached. Jane McGonigal (2012), author of *Reality is Broken*, poses an interesting question: we often think of games as escapist, a way to retreat from reality, but what if we viewed games more thoughtfully, as a way to find a stronger sense of community, more engaging work, and meaningful life? McGonigal argues that games can build connections with the people around us, enhance our life experiences, and even make a difference in the world around us. She shares examples like Free Rice, a trivia game that donates rice for every question correctly answered, and Cruel 2 Be Kind, a game that encourages you to "kill" other people with acts of kindness. In *Making Democracy Fun*, Josh Lerner (2014) explores using game mechanics to make democracy more participatory. He explains that when people play a game, they become more interested in the game's issues. Thus, as players learn and become more aware, they are more likely to participate in politics and the community. Lerner cites an example where teams collaborated to create an engaging presentation to compete for community funding. Teams presented all their projects and then voted on the presentations and projects that they felt should be funded. Another example had participants moving puzzle pieces around on a map that represented low-income housing that the city wished to redesign. Working in neighborhood teams they evaluated what each person wanted and needed and then used the interactive puzzle map to lay out their new neighborhood. Both Lerner and McGonigal view games as a way for participants to collaborate and engage in their world. If we view games in this same way, games become a space where human rights concepts can be explored and students can take their learning from the world of the game to the real world.

Schools have a history of exploring with gamification, using game ideas in other contexts, to engage and motivate students. Some schools have experimented with using badge systems to reward students; they compete to earn badges such as Master of Triangles, Homework Hero, or Lord of Calligraphy. These badges reflect academic goals and students must complete certain "missions" to earn them. Other game mechanics used in schools target behavior; students can +1 if they work collaboratively as a team, +1 if they bring all their materials, or +1 if they help clean up the classroom (Seixas et al., 2016). Other schools have focused on the game mechanics of leaderboards. It is not uncommon for schools to encourage students and teachers to set goals for their learning, but leaderboards shift this to a different viewpoint. With leaderboards, participants choose their own goals; they decide what placement on the leaderboard they are striving for, and they work to achieve their desired position (Landers et al., 2017). Quest to Learn School in New York City uses gamification on a grand scale. Students don't earn traditional grades, instead, they level up until they achieve expert status in a subject. The assignments are phrased as missions. Some are even secret missions that are hidden around the school and if a student finds them, they can complete the secret mission to earn bonus points. Students create profiles to advertise their skills and expertise. Lessons and skills culminate in a two-week intense "boss level" where students collaborate using cross-disciplinary skills to tackle an epic challenge.

There are already a few games that specifically target human rights learning. The United Kingdom Human Rights Act of 1998 has five core principles: fairness, respect, equality, dignity, and autonomy. A group created a game called *FREDA Challenge* which draws on those five principles. The game is designed to be played by people with intellectual disabilities and their caregivers. People with intellectual disabilities have historically experienced abuse from care systems and institutions, so the game hopes to raise human rights awareness. Playing the game facilitates increased knowledge about human rights and people with intellectual disabilities (Montenegro & Greenhill, 2014). Another example is the game *ICED*, which stands for *I Can End Deportation*. In this online game, players choose an avatar and try and negotiate life in New York City without getting caught. The choices that players make in the game resemble their ability to exercise free will and agency in the real world; however, the game always ends in capture. Players are put in ethical dilemmas and forced to make difficult decisions. The game was designed by the group Breakthrough to challenge xenophobia and harsh immigration policies (Amaya, 2015).

Human Rights Education Game

Thinking about different approaches to human rights education and the transformative power of games, I set out to design a new human rights education game that could be played in elementary schools. The balance of this chapter shares the process that I took to design, playtest, and refine the game. I want to make it clear that when I started designing this game, I wasn't even sure it would work out. I am certainly not an expert in game design, but I had some experience as a teacher building games to use in my classroom. I first started using games in math class, mostly using decks of cards or race-to-the-end style games that encouraged students to practice their math skills as they moved along the path within the game. But beyond that I needed guidance, so I turned to *Clockwork Game Design* by Keith Burgun (2015). Burgun begins by defining what a game is. His definition has three essential components: decision-making, incomplete information, and a goal. Games fit into the broad category of interactive systems, which Burgun breaks down into four categories: toys, puzzles, contests, and games. Toys have rules, but not goals. Puzzles have a binary goal – solve it or not, but once they are solved then they lose value. Contests have a goal and are measured, considering races or a spelling bee. Games take elements from the other types of systems and combine them. A key element of games is that they force players to make decisions. Burgun explains that decisions fall somewhere between guesses and solutions—with a guess you have essentially no information, whereas with a solution you essentially have all the information. Burgun also introduced the idea of emergent vs componential complexity, where componential complexity comes from the initial rules and setup of the game. They are in place at the start, added to the game by the designers. Emergent complexity comes from the unique situations that arise from decisions that players make in the game and are driven by the players, not by the designer.

Designing the Game Board

Now with this new understanding of what a game is, I started to think about what a human rights game could look like. I began by thinking about the game board and what that could look like. I knew that I wanted to emphasize that human rights violations take place across the world. I was also pretty sure that I didn't want to do a race-to-the-end style game. I firmly believe that creativity and collaboration are essential pieces to working to address human rights violations and I felt as if the game presented only one path to work towards new solutions that undermined the opportunities for students to create solutions. Additionally, it felt counter to the ideas of human rights to have players compete against each other. To me, in a game about human rights, the players had to work together, to emphasize collaboration, respect, and collective responsibility. Ultimately, I went with the idea that the game board should be the world. Players would work together against the board. Figure 2.1 shows a draft of the game board. The world is divided into 6 regions and 18 subregions rather than following existing political or geographic borders.

Figure 2.1. Initial Draft of the Crisis Game Board

Characters and the Theme of the Game

With the game board roughly designed, I next thought about characters, the types of decisions players would have to make and who were the players of this game. For this, I turned to Michael Moore who wrote *Basics of Game Design* (2011). I had two big takeaways from Moore's work. First, Moore addresses the fun and less fun elements of games. Some things are very fun like finding treasure, driving cars or planes, solving puzzles, and interacting with characters. Other tasks are less fun like buying or selling objects, bookkeeping, and inventory management. But often games require players to do both things. The other idea that Moore introduced was storytelling and character. Burgun (2015) also explores different traits of characters. Moore and Burgun share that players are invested in the game if they are invested in the story of the characters. My first thought was to take real human rights violations and create characters connected to the story. I thought there was a lot of potential for the game to tell an interesting story of human rights violations and to harness the power of storytelling. But one of the challenges is that I felt the game should be able to tell multiple stories, both because everyone involved in a human rights violation has their own story, and because the game needed to be able to be played more than once.

Around this time, I attended a workshop with the University of Connecticut Neag School of Education professor Steven Slota, who talked about developing educational games. Slota talked through the design process and shared the importance of having clear educational outcomes. I have two educational outcomes for this game: first, I wanted players to learn about real human rights violations across the world; second, I wanted players to understand that addressing human rights violations is complex and requires collaboration and creative thinking. I wanted my players to have to work together, instead of competing to win the game.

The game needed a guiding theme that I could use to craft the story of the game and the learning objectives. I decided that the game would explore slavery. Learning about slavery in the United States is an elementary learning standard, but it was important that the game encourage students to think about slavery in a global sense.

Game Mechanics

The world of my game board is defined into 18 subregions, which are grouped into 6 regions (see Figure 2.2). The regions generally do not reflect real political boundaries because human rights violations are not often bounded by political boundaries, and I wanted to continue to reinforce the idea that human rights violations affect everyone across the globe.

Figure 2.2. Final Verion of the Crisis Game Board

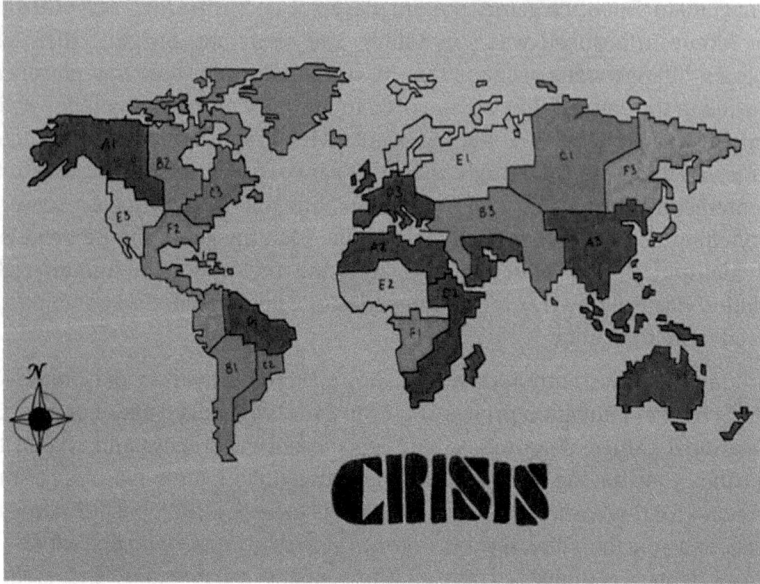

Playing the Game

Once the world was divided into regions, I began researching historic and modern facts about slavery that corresponded to each region of the game board. These facts about slavery became the card deck for the game. Players would draw a card and each card would have a fact about slavery. They would read the fact and place a "violation marker" in the corresponding region on the game board. See Figure 2.3 for a sample of cards in the game deck.

Figure 2.3. Sample Human Rights Game Cards

During WWII, the Japanese military enslaved thousands of Korean and Chinese women as "comfort women"	In 2018, there were an estimated 1,386,000 victims of slavery in Nigeria	The first slaves arrived in the colonies at Jamestown in 1619. By 1790 the number of slaves in Virginia was 293,000
Put a marker in Zone F3	Put a marker in Zone E2	Put a marker in Zone C3

One of the concepts that Schell (2015) explores is balance in games. One of the aspects of balance is basic vs. strategic actions. Basic actions are simple actions that players take. Strategic actions are actions that players plan and take a few moves to realize. Knowing that the players would work together I wanted the potential for both. So as they responded to human rights violations, they could choose either the basic action that was simplest or work towards a more strategic action that had a greater payoff but took a few moves to make happen. Schell also explores balancing skill and chance. Chance is random, but skill removes the influence of fate. Choice is also something that Schell (2015) emphasizes. Players make choices and the choices impact the outcome of the game. Choice points are moments where the choice a player makes drastically impacts the outcome. Schell advocates for a balance of choice and desire.

I settled on two different pathways to address human rights violations: Military and Diplomatic. Military action was meant to mirror how countries send troops to a place in crisis to restore peace. To take military action, one player had to be in the same region where they wished to address a human rights violation. That player then rolled a single die, and another player rolled a die on behalf of the board. If the game player's die had a higher number, they could remove a human rights violation marker from that subregion. If the board's die was higher, another violation marker was added to the region. Diplomatic action was meant to mirror actions like drafting a treaty or hosting a conference. To take diplomatic action players must collect two diplomatic task cards and assemble all players in the region where they want to take diplomatic action. Diplomatic action led to the removal of two human rights violation markers in a region.

So each player's turn had three parts: 1) draw a human rights card and place a human rights violation marker, 2) take military or diplomatic action if they wanted to, and 3) move to a different region if they wanted to.

Winning and Losing

It took me a while to figure out how "winning the game" would work. Burgun (2015) explains point systems, time limits, and health status bars in different games, but none of them really seemed to fit my objectives. Human rights violations are ongoing and there is always the potential for new violations to occur in the world. I wanted players to realize that addressing human rights is an ongoing challenge and an ongoing need. Because of this, it was difficult to figure out what it meant to "win the game." Eventually, I came up with the idea for a team status bar that represents your team's ability to recognize and respond to human rights violations.

So the players would work together to move up the status bar to win the game. Based on the outcomes of the military or diplomatic action described above, the status level changed. Taking successful military action would allow the team to move up one status level. Taking successful diplomatic action would allow the team to move up two status levels. When the team reaches level 8, they win the game, but there may still be ongoing human rights violations on the board, emphasizing that there is still work that must be done. Burgun (2015) also addresses moral choices in games. Players understand that they are playing with a game world and that when they kill someone in a game world it is not the same as killing someone in the real world.

Another idea that Schell (2105) explores is the abstract nature of time. I wanted there to be a mechanism that placed some time limit on how long teams had to respond to any individual human rights violation. I created a "crisis tracker" or "human rights violation watch" with five spots where players would place the human rights cards that they had drawn. With only five spots, it meant that players had five turns to address each human rights violation. If they didn't address the human rights violation in five turns it was placed face down on the top of the deck amplifying the violation by adding another marker to that region on the next turn.

I had already decided on reaching team status level 8 as a winning condition, but I wanted players to be able to lose. Thus, if any region gets 6 human rights violations, then the players lose and the game is won. Thinking back to the *ICED* video game (Amaya, 2015), in which players always lose, I considered if I wanted players to always lose this game. While this would reinforce the idea that human rights violations are ongoing, I felt that the tone was too somber. I wanted players to have a sense of hope that human rights violations could be addressed and corrected. Schell (2015) also talks about the experience of playing the game and what emotions players feel as they play. I wanted players to feel sad and concerned, a sense of panic, but also empowered. I figured that information about actual human rights violations would lead to sadness and concern. I hoped that as the game progressed and they saw the number of violations piling up across the board they would feel the panic and urgency of action. And I hoped that as they worked together, they would feel empowered and hopeful for the future.

Playtesting and Revising the Game

With the basics of the game settled, I played the game with three different groups of students; two fifth-grade groups and a sixth-grade group. As I watched the kids play the game it was clear that they really enjoyed it and were engaged in the game. But it was also clear that some of the elements didn't work in the way that I had envisioned them working. Some of the players were really interested in the facts that were on the cards, while others just skipped to the bottom to find out where to place a marker on the board. This suggested that the game mechanics were not fully realizing the learning objective of teaching students about real-world human rights violations.

As I reflected on their conversations it was clear to me that the game had potential, but things need to be refined to fully realize the learning objectives. Students seem more focused on removing markers from the board instead of talking about the issues. I needed to think about more ways to encourage conversation. Also, I needed to revise the team status level and crisis tracker. Further, I had been thinking about humanitarian aid efforts and wanted to think about a way to bring those into the game. So with my first round of playtesting completed and some good feedback, I began revisions.

The biggest revision I made was adding a humanitarian response to human rights violations. I created a set of five humanitarian cards: design a monument, write a letter, write a poem, lead a protest, and create a piece of artwork. When the team decides that they want to take humanitarian action they select the card that they wish to complete and then they work as a team to complete the action on the card. If they choose to design a monument their monument must include the location, a sketch of the monument, a title, and an artist's statement. If they choose to lead a protest, they must write down the aims of their protest, what action the protesters will take, and where the protest will occur. Once they complete their humanitarian action, they can remove three violation markers and move up two status levels on the team status bar.

Conclusion

Human Rights Education seeks to create a global culture of human rights and develop citizens who are aware of human rights and have the skills to promote and protect human rights. I wanted to create a game that would position students to take an active role in their learning about human rights and also challenge them to grapple with some of the decisions and challenges that accompany addressing human rights in the real world. This chapter shares the inception, creation, and refining of a game that introduces and explores human rights concepts in an upper elementary classroom. A key element of the game is collaboration and working together. The game challenges students to think about global slavery and the impact of different decisions. The three different responses to slavery: military action, diplomatic action, or humanitarian aid require different skills and prompt players to discuss and evaluate different responses to human rights violations. Throughout this chapter, I have highlighted not only the process of developing the game but also some important considerations about game design. It is my hope that by sharing the process of design and revision that this game went through; others will recognize human rights as a potential area for game-based approaches to learning and designing their own games.

References

Amaya, H. (2015). *ICED: Videogames in the battle between the citizen and the human.* Popular Communication, 13:2, 158-169, DOI: 10.1080/15405702.2015.1021465

Amnesty International. (2018). *Write 4 rights 2018 – A Human rights education toolkit for educators.*

Asia Pacific Human Rights Information Center. (2003). *Human rights lesson plans for southeast Asian schools.* Reuan Kaew.

Bickmore, K. (2014). Peacebuilding dialogue pedagogies in Canadian classrooms. *Curriculum Inquiry, 44*(4), 553–582. doi: 10.1111/curi.12056

Burgun, K. (2015). *Clockwork game design.* CRC Press.

Landers, R. N., Bauer, K. N., & Callan, R. C. (2017). Gamification of task performance with leaderboards: A goal setting experiment. *Computers in Human Behavior, 71,* 508–515. doi: 10.1016/j.chb.2015.08.008

Lerner, J. (2014). *Making democracy fun: How game design can empower citizens and transform politics.* Cambridge: MIT Press.

McGonigal, J. (2012). *Reality is broken: Why games make us better and how they can change the world.* Vintage.

Montenegro, M., & Greenhill, B. (2014, September 8). *Evaluating 'FREDA Challenge': A coproduced human rights board game in services for people with intellectual disabilities.* Wiley Online Library. https://onlinelibrary.wiley.com/doi/10.1111/jar.12124

Moore, Michael. (2011). *Basics of game design.* CRC Press.

National Council for the Social Studies. (2015) Human rights education: A necessity for effective social and civic learning. NCSS Position Statement. *Social Education, 79*(3), 161–164.

Padilla, L. (2011). Notes from the field: Implementing human rights education in service-learning courses. *Societies Without Borders, 6*(2), 92-108.

Schell, J. (2015). *The art of game design: A deck of lenses.* Schell Games.

Seixas, L. D. R., Gomes, A. S., & Filho, I. J. D. M. (2016). Effectiveness of gamification in the engagement of students. *Computers in Human Behavior, 58,* 48–63. doi: 10.1016/j.chb.2015.11.021

Sohcot, S., Sebastian Chang, E., Crowell, S., McEvoy Spero, A., & Rodriguez Sofaer, V. (2019). *The world as it could be human rights education program.* Almeda County Deputy Sheriff's Activities League. www.theworldasitcouldbe.org

United Nations. (1948). *Universal declaration of human rights.* www.un.org/en/udhrbook/pdf/udhr_booklet_en_web.pdf

United Nations Publication. (2004). *Teaching human rights practical activities for primary and secondary schools.* Geneva.

Chapter 3

Gamification in Education: How Gaming Can Be Used as a Tool to Drive Student Engagement and Increase Learning Outcomes for Children with Autism Spectrum Disorder (ASD)

Jessica Wythe

Birmingham City University

Abstract: Wythe takes on engagement of students with autism spectrum disorder (ASD), looking at gamification strategies to help students want to participate in the learning. Two studies are presented here to show different strategies of employing gamification to knowledge.

Keywords: autism spectrum disorder; gamification

***

Introduction

Is gamification the key to pupil engagement? This chapter explores the impacts of game-based learning in primary schools in the United Kingdom (UK) for children in Key Stage 1 (ages 5-7) and Key Stage 2 (ages 7-11) with autism spectrum disorder (ASD).

Gamification refers to the use of game design elements and principles in non-game contexts with the goal of enhancing engagement, motivation, and participation. When utilized and integrated effectively in various environments, such as school classrooms or workplace contexts, gamification can have several benefits, particularly in relation to engagement, motivation, and progress (Brigham, 2015). Moreover, monopolizing gamification teaching strategies in an educational context can enhance pupils' motivation and engagement in complex subjects like maths (Brigham, 2015; Kim et al., 2017). Similarly, Kolb's theory of Experiential Learning (1984) reinforces that children learn best through physically experiencing learning concepts. According to Kolb, the process of learning through experience means that children are more likely to retain and comprehend new concepts than if they are disengaged (Kolb, 1984). Retrospectively, practical, and creative pedagogical strategies and learning opportunities are often utilized within primary education to enhance pupils' motivation and engagement.

The prominence of electronic gaming platforms has significantly increased in the twenty-first century. Many online games had record-high player numbers during the Coronavirus pandemic in response to the social distancing and lockdown guidelines, meaning children were spending more time at home. Following the initial school closures in 2020, virtual learning platforms, such as Zoom and Microsoft Teams, were introduced and utilized to facilitate home education (Begum et al., 2021; Paudel, 2021). Consequently, blended learning opportunities are becoming increasingly more popular in primary school classrooms, such as the use of technology in the classroom and a balance of child-led and teacher-led learning opportunities and experiences.

With the increase of technology and multi-modal pedagogical strategies in mainstream learning contexts, this study combined the relationship between gamification and blended learning to establish whether these can be used as tools to increase learning engagement and motivation in Key Stage 1 and Key Stage 2 mainstream education classrooms in the UK.

Autism Spectrum Disorder

Autism spectrum disorder (ASD) is a neurological disorder that can cause challenges to communication, social interaction, behavior, and independence along with developmental impairments (Boucher, 2017; Wearmouth, 2017). As it is a spectrum disorder, individuals with ASD may differ widely in terms of how the characteristics of ASD are presented. ASD can mildly or more severely impact social interaction, emotional and communication skills, and behavior and cause cognitive delays (Campisi et al., 2018; Frederickson & Cline, 2015). Research substantiates that ASD is one of the most common developmental disabilities in children and young people. Statistics published by the National Autistic Society (2020) reveal that one in 100 people has a form of ASD, and there are around 700,000 autistic adults and children in the UK.

The prevalence of ASD within society makes it a current issue within education. Consequently, it is of great importance that education professionals meet their statutory obligations regarding promoting inclusion in practice and are knowledgeable of how to support and appropriately implement strategies or interventions to meet the potentially complex needs of children or young people with ASD (Kodak et al., 2017; Wearmouth & Butler, 2020).

Children with ASD often experience difficulty maintaining attention and focus when learning new concepts. They often display low levels of engagement, limiting the learning opportunities for their typically developing peers (Odom et al., 2010; Ruble & Robson, 2007). Additionally, the research emphasizes how children with ASD may have obsessions, special interests, and habits (Courchesne et al., 2020; Klin et al., 2007). One of the defining symptoms of ASD is repetitive behaviors and restricted interests (Hodges et al., 2020). Games such as Minecraft can be effective for children with autism in making new friends and developing social and cognitive skills (Rutkin, 2016).

Research affirms that stimulating learner interests can promote and increase learning through increasing attention, focus, and engagement (Harackiewicz et al., 2016). If children are interested in learning something, such as if they are being taught in an engaging way if their individual interests are integrated into the planned provision, or if there are cognitive or hands-on learning experiences involved, then they are more likely to be engaged with the learning and motivated to participate in the learning experience, meaning that they are more likely to attain the intended learning benefits for the planned provision (Birbili & Melpomeni, 2008; Gunn & Delafield-Butt, 2016).

In the context of children with autism, high-interest learning opportunities can facilitate a richer understanding of taught concepts and increase learning participation and engagement (Dunst et al., 2010). This study explores how online games and gamification can impact learning engagement, motivation, and participation for children with ASD in mainstream education in the United Kingdom.

Research Questions and Methodology

The research questions that shape this chapter are as follows:

- How can gaming characters and concepts be incorporated into education?
- Can gamification enhance learning engagement for children with ASD?
- What are the implications of game-based learning for children with ASD?

These research questions have been addressed through a study that consists of two separate interviews with a total of five primary school teachers in the UK and two comparative observations of how children with ASD respond to standardized learning opportunities and learning opportunities involving gamification elements. A process of thematic analysis revealed that gamification could enhance and increase learning engagement and motivation for children with ASD.

Findings: Primary School Teacher Interviews

The teachers interviewed shared how they utilize popular characters and games, such as Roblox and Minecraft, in their planning and provision to attain and sustain focus and interest. Additionally, they use opportunities for children to learn through gamification strategies, such as utilizing competition as a tool for engagement and motivation, and have seen overwhelmingly positive results, particularly with learners with ASD. However, many instructors identified gamification and game-based pedagogy challenges, such as time implications and the dangers of children becoming too dependent on games and technology.

The following quotations are from the interviews with primary school teachers as they discuss the role of gaming in driving learning engagement and academic outcomes for children with ASD.

The Benefits of Gamification Strategies in Relation to Engagement and Motivation

Gamification can significantly elevate engagement and motivation in education by transforming traditional learning experiences into dynamic and interactive journeys. By incorporating game elements into educational activities, lesson plans, and learning experiences that stimulate individual learner interests, all students, particularly those with ASD, are motivated to participate actively and progress in their learning. Integrating gamification strategies within education encourages students to fully engage in the learning process and reach their full academic potential, as the competitive nature of games fosters a sense of excitement and achievement.

> "Children love a game; they all have a drive to win. I use competition in the classroom a lot to motivate the learners, particularly with subjects like maths, where the children are not always fully focused. Competition and rewards are a good way to keep my class motivated and on track, especially toward the end of the school day when the class energy starts to dip. This works well for children with autism especially, as they know what is expected of them, academically and behaviourally. Sometimes when I use competition though, children can get upset and overwhelmed, particularly if they don't 'win', so I am not over-reliant on competition."
> – Teacher 1.

"A good example of using games to promote learning is in my science lessons. I never really engaged with science at school, and it was one of my worst subjects in primary and secondary school, and because of my poor learning experiences, I am determined to make my own science lessons a lot more engaging. My science lessons are structured, but I use gaming tools like roleplay and competition to increase engagement and participation, which I find works well for all learners, especially those with autism. I know how dependent on routine some children can be, so I always assign roles at the start of the lesson to pairs of children, such as setting up the equipment, handing out the goggles and lab aprons, things like that. I also really like to get the children to work in pairs or in small groups as that's when the best learning happens, I find. The children kind of just bounce [ideas] off each other!" – Teacher 3.

"I also like giving the children tasks to do in pairs or small groups. I sometimes set different tasks to different groups, so that the element of competition is still there, but then as each group has its own goals, there are no winners or losers as all tasks need to be completed. Even something like tidying up the classroom at the end of the day, or a scavenger hunt for a geography lesson where each group has to collect information about a different country. I find that my classes are almost motivated by each other, as well as by the game-based strategies that I use in the classroom." – Teacher 1.

The primary school teachers interviewed discussed that using gamification strategies in the classroom enhances student engagement and cultivates a positive and motivating learning context that promotes active participation, learning focus, and a deeper understanding of educational content. The teachers affirm that the benefits of gamification strategies concerning engagement and motivation are prominent for all learners, but the implications are amplified for children and young people with ASD.

Conclusively, gamification strategies in the classroom have extensive learning progress and engagement affordances. They offer a versatile and practical approach to enhancing engagement and motivation in the classroom–concepts that can be translated to any phase of education. By leveraging the motivational aspects inherent in games and competitions, gamification strategies can make activities more enjoyable, rewarding, and ultimately more successful concerning academic outcomes, learning comprehension, and progress.

The Role of Technology as a Tool to Promote Learning Engagement

Technological change underpins many of the developments in education and society. Technology plays a pivotal role in promoting learning engagement by offering innovative and interactive solutions catering to diverse learning styles. It serves as a dynamic and versatile educational tool to enhance learning engagement by aligning with student interests and offering personalized and interactive educational experiences. When effectively integrated into educational contexts and aligned with curriculum concepts and content, technology can create a more engaging and inclusive learning environment and enhance learning and skill development among learners with ASD.

"Technology is a great way to get children engaged in learning. I think because technology is so 'normal' in today's society, many children have their own mobile phones, or they have a computer or iPad at home. So, when we introduce technology in the classroom, there is that familiarity, and they can make the link between the classroom and home." – Teacher 4.

"Technology is used in my classroom every day, some days more than others. I am lucky to have an interactive whiteboard in my classroom which I use several times a day with the children, I have used it for teaching new material, such as phonics, quizzing the children on previously taught content, things like maths games, and also YouTube videos. My class are fans of 'Come Outside' [UK TV Show] which I often integrate into teaching as it has educational elements, such as the dangers of fire and how different inventions are made." – Teacher 5.

"I find that the children in my class with autism are a lot more engaged in the lessons where technology is used. We have our IT (Information Technology) lessons in the computer suites, but we have recently been using iPads and laptops in the classroom for other subjects too. I did a project in literacy where the children designed a monster on paper and then wrote a descriptive paragraph about the monster. Then, the following week, they used an app on the iPads where they could draw and create their monster using different colors and textures, there was some extraordinary work from my class which the children were rightfully so proud of." – Teacher 4.

"There was…an activity that I did with my Year 6 group last year where I split them into groups of 4, and they each had to research a different mountain using the iPads and books around the classroom. Then, they used this information to create a poster for each mountain. I only had 1 child in this group who had been diagnosed with autism, but he engaged really well with this activity as he was 'in charge' of the laptop – he would search the terms and keywords that his group gave to him and collate the information onto a piece of paper. It was an effective way to make sure that he was involved in the learning." – Teacher 5.

"Technology and games can be a great way to support learning if used correctly. After lunch, I get the children to do a round of 'Just Dance'. The videos I use are recorded gameplay videos that I have found on YouTube–I play the video on the big screen at the front of the classroom, and the children dance along and join in. I often let the children choose which song they want to dance to as well. They love this part of the day and, of course, it keeps them fit and healthy and ready to focus on the afternoon learning." – Teacher 3.

"I think it can be challenging to have a balance of technology and hands-on learning. I only tend to use hand-held technology in the class maybe once or twice a week. I don't want the children to become overly reliant on it, especially the learners who have autism or special educational needs. My class does enjoy playing games though, I even make parts of the day like getting their bags and coats at the end of the day into a game. For example, who can get their coats first, the boys or girls? Or which table can get their coats and bags the most quietly?" – Teacher 1.

"I use a similar approach in my classroom at the end of the day, especially if we have five minutes left until home time. I like the 21 game, where the children have to shout a number each and make it to 21, but if two children shout the same number, then they must start again. They also like the supermarket game, where you say, 'I went to the supermarket and bought an apple…' and then the next person repeats it, but adds a new item starting with B, then we see how far through the alphabet we can get. I make the 'end of day' game a part of the daily routine." – Teacher 4.

The primary school teachers discussed their experiences of integrating educational technology in the classroom and its benefits for children and young people, particularly those with ASD. Technology plays a crucial role as a tool to promote learning engagement for children with ASD through facilitating and promoting a structured and predictable learning environment, which is often integral for children and young people with ASD who benefit from routine and consistency.

Additionally, the primary school teachers affirmed that technology makes educational content more engaging and immersive, which supports children with ASD in developing integral skills and academic knowledge in a way that is both enjoyable and accessible. Technology not only fosters individualized and interest-based learning experiences and increases learning engagement, participation, and motivation but also enables and facilitates teachers to adjust learning interventions and assess and monitor learning progress to support the individual and sometimes complex needs of each child with ASD.

The Relationship between Creative Pedagogical Strategies and Learning Engagement

Creative pedagogical strategies involve the application of imaginative and innovative approaches to teaching and learning to increase learning engagement and participation and, consequently, enhance learning outcomes and progress. Creative approaches to teaching and learning improve the quality of teaching and learning engagement and contribute to a positive and enriching educational experience for children and young people through carefully planned innovative learning opportunities. The relationship between creative pedagogical strategies and learning engagement for children with ASD is particularly prominent, given the diverse learning styles and spectrum of individual needs associated with autism.

"I think using hands-on learning approaches do have the best results and using gaming strategies does genuinely increase learning participation. You know, if you have planned a really fun learning experience that the children are interested in, then they are going to want to take part. If the children are focused and interested, then you will get their best work than if you had given them a standardized maths worksheet, for example, with twenty multiplication questions on it. I empathize that teachers do not always have the confidence or time capacity to plan such innovative learning experiences though, and we are bound by outcomes and the curriculum." – Teacher 3.

"There is much more of a focus on teaching the children specific concepts and then assessing their understanding. I would love to make my teaching more fun for the children, but there simply aren't enough hours in the day, particularly during the days when I am on my own with twenty-five children, and three of those have special educational needs and require additional support anyway." – Teacher 2.

"I try to use gaming-based strategies as much as I can within my planning and provision, but ...I am unable to use them as much as I would desire. I see the benefits of gamification, especially with the children in my class who have autistic spectrum disorders – they are more likely to take part in the lesson and be focused and engaged. At the end of the day, a bored or disengaged child is a lot less likely to give a lesson their full attention and, in turn, this will impact what they take away from the lesson, I think." – Teacher 5.

The primary school teachers discussed the affordances of incorporating creative and gaming-based elements into their teaching and planned provision, such as interactive games and hands-on teaching methods, in capturing the interest of children with ASD and, consequently, promoting learning engagement and knowledge acquisition and retention. If utilized and integrated within the classroom to support and enhance taught curriculum content, creative pedagogical approaches, such as gamification strategies, facilitate tailored teaching approaches that consider the unique and often complex learning needs of children and young people with ASD. Furthermore, the emphasis on the flexibility and learner-centered nature of creative pedagogy allows educators to adapt their approaches based on each child's individual needs and responses, fostering a personalized, positive, and supportive learning atmosphere that enhances overall learning engagement and participation.

Moreover, the teachers discussed their positive experiences of integrating creative and innovative teaching strategies into the classroom. They asserted the benefits of utilizing gamification methods to attain and sustain learner interest and motivation. Creative strategies, including technology, games, hands-on learning experiences, and art-based activities, enable primary school teachers to present, deliver, and convey information in ways that resonate with the strengths and preferences of children with ASD. Correspondingly, children and young people are more likely to be actively involved, motivated, and excited about their learning if information and curriculum concepts are presented and taught in a creative and memorable way that stimulates them to be actively interested in and focused on what they are doing and learning about in the classroom.

Using Individual Interests to Increase Learning Engagement for Children with ASD

Leveraging and integrating individual interests into planned provision and the learning environment is a highly effective and powerful strategy to increase learning engagement for children with ASD. Recognizing and incorporating a child's specific interests into educational activities, lessons, and learning experiences not only captures their attention and sustains their focus in the planned provision but also creates a more personally meaningful learning experience and increases the likelihood that they will be more focused on their learning and development. Through aligning educational content with the child's interests, teachers promote and stimulate intrinsic motivation, making the learning process more enjoyable and relevant for children and young people and, in turn, increasing motivation, participation, and learning progress.

> "I tend to use children's interests a lot in all aspects of my teaching. In the classroom, I use characters such as Dan TDM [Minecraft YouTube Gamer] on my display boards, so the children have that familiarity. Then with my teaching, I often use similar characters within my lessons–for instance, I did an activity once where the children wrote a diary entry for a character who was stuck in a Fortnite Battle Royale world, which they really engaged with. These approaches work really well for the children in my class who have autism as they are familiar with the characters and games that I use, and I feel that these links mean that they are more engaged with what is being taught." – Teacher 2.

> "Gamification in the classroom can have significant benefits, and I do believe that more attention should be given to how new concepts and subjects are taught in the classroom, rather than what needs to be taught. The curriculum in the UK is very prescriptive I find, which is good to an extent as it means that all children are learning the same content, but I would make significant changes to the guidance concerning how the curriculum content is taught – including more interesting teaching strategies. Who knows, maybe this creative and more innovative approach is what is missing from the education system?" – Teacher 3.

It is imperative for teachers and educators to observe and understand each child's unique interests and learning preferences and integrate these into lesson plans and activities. The primary school teachers discussed the affordances of incorporating individual learner interests, creative pedagogical strategies, and gaming-based elements into their teaching and planned provision to increase learning engagement and participation and academic progress and outcomes. This innovative approach to education not only enhances learning engagement for children and young people with ASD, but it fosters a positive association with learning, creating a supportive educational environment that stimulates exploration and active participation, ultimately contributing to a more prosperous and enriching learning experience. The individualized and learner-centered nature of using individual interests to increase learning engagement for children with ASD enhances learning engagement. Moreover, this inclusive approach respects the child's preferences, making the learning experience more enjoyable and relative to positive academic outcomes for children with ASD.

A Key Stage 1 Case Study—Teaching Mathematics through Game Elements and Gaming-Based Interests (Year 3)

This observation was conducted in a mixed-ability Year 3 classroom (ages 7-8) in a mainstream school in the UK. The classroom had twenty-six children, a class teacher, and a 1:1 teaching assistant—the class teacher disclosed that the class had a learner who was diagnosed with high-functioning autism spectrum disorder, and who had extensive interests in the game Minecraft. The lesson observed was in the afternoon, and it was the final lesson of the day. The teacher was teaching multiplication, and this was the second corresponding mathematics lesson that had a multiplication focus.

The lesson commenced with a recap of the previous learning—a group quiz where the questions were presented on the interactive whiteboard at the front of the classroom. All the children were sat on the carpet. The quiz followed a traditional question-and-answer structure where the class received a point for each question that was answered correctly. The class was all extremely engaged with the activity and were all keen to answer a question; there were instances where behavioral norms were forgotten, such as putting your hand up to answer. In the excitement of the non-traditional assessment strategy, the teacher did have to stop the quiz on two occasions to manage the class behavior. However, the quiz proved an effective strategy for recapping previous learning, and it helped the children to recall previously taught information and knowledge. All children in the class answered at least one question, including the child with ASD, who confidently answered their question and was delighted to receive a point towards the class's total. The class got every question right and the teacher rewarded the class with a promise of 'golden time' on the corresponding Friday—a positive behavior management strategy used in many primary schools where there is no formal curriculum teaching on Friday afternoons and instead, the class teacher organizes the classroom and the outdoor space with a range of different activities, such as arts and crafts, jigsaws, play dough, iPads, chalk, and balls.

The next part of the lesson plan consisted of an activity where each table was given a sheet of paper with ten different multiplication questions. The child with ASD was sat at a table with their 1:1 teaching assistant. The teaching assistant led the activity—the first question was 4 multiplied by 2. They used blocks of Lego to model working out the answer to the equation and used links to the Minecraft game: "If Dr. Trayaurus [character from DanTDM's Minecraft gaming series on YouTube] had four blocks of TNT, and then had another four blocks of coal—how many blocks would he have all together?" The child counted the Lego blocks that the teaching assistant had gathered and confidently answered that the answer was eight. "But the TNT would blow up the coal!" they exclaimed, making links back to the Minecraft game. "But the sum was multiplied by two, so we needed two different types of material," the teaching assistant replied, "can you have a go at the next question?." The following question was three multiplied by five—the child counted out five Lego blocks and explained that these are iron blocks, as "the TNT can't blow up iron." Next, they gathered another five blocks and said that these were TNT blocks. Finally, they gathered five green blocks and explained that these were emerald blocks. "So how many blocks does Dr. Trayaurus have?" the teaching assistant prompted, ensuring that the child stayed on task. The child confidently counted the blocks and stacked them into a tower. "We have fifteen!" he exclaimed confidently.

This was an example of how everyday resources, such as Lego blocks, can be effective tools in stimulating individual interests and teaching curriculum concepts in an engaging way that sustains learner attention. The links to the child's interests in Minecraft meant that they were more engaged in participating in the mathematics activity. This activity helped them to develop their knowledge and understanding of multiplication. Additionally, the use of the quiz at the start of the lesson was an effective way to assess the pre-existing knowledge of the class—if there were any incorrect questions during this quiz, then the teacher could have used this information to plan for future mathematics instruction. The use of a non-traditional and prescriptive assessment strategy and the use of gamification-based strategies such as competition and the use of points meant that all the children wanted to participate and try their best, in comparison to a traditional written or spoken assessment method where the learners may have been more disengaged and less willing to put up their hands and volunteer to answer the questions.

Conclusion and Recommendations

This chapter concludes that although gamification has some challenges and limitations in education, the implications of utilizing gaming-based strategies in a mainstream education classroom in the United Kingdom can have extensive benefits for learning and engagement, particularly for students with ASD. The research conducted explores the benefits of gamification in education and demonstrates that the implications of game-based learning for children with ASD are overwhelmingly positive (Brigham, 2015). Through interviewing primary school teachers and observing how children and young people with ASD interact with lessons and learning experiences that utilize gaming characters and concepts and gamification strategies to engage the children in the learning process, it is evident that such strategies can enhance learning engagement for children and young people with ASD. Furthermore, this research affirms the educational and learning benefits of teachers utilizing hands-on and exciting teaching strategies aligned with the children's interests in the classroom, such as using popular gaming characters and tools such as competition and races. In turn, the learners are anticipated to be more engaged with the learning and motivated to participate in the learning experience, meaning that they are more likely to attain the intended learning benefits for the planned provision (Birbili & Melpomeni, 2008; Gunn & Delafield-Butt, 2016). It is imperative that teachers consider the individual interests of the learners in their class and have an awareness of popular culture in relation to gaming and mass media. This is prevalent with children with ASD, as it is common for them to have special interests, and habits, such as an interest in a particular game (Courchesne et al., 2020). Such information can be invaluable in the classroom during the planning and provision processes, and it is reasonable to assume that it will have extensive positive implications for student engagement participation and learning outcomes.

References

Begum, M. J., Haider, N., Baig, W. A. & Eqbal, K. (2021) Impact of Covid-19 Pandemic on quality of education. *International Journal of Applied Research, 7*(5), 4-7. https://doi.org/10.22271/allresearch.2021.v7.i5a.8534

Birbili, M. & Melpomeni, T. (2008) *Identifying children's interests and planning learning experiences: Challenging some taken-for-granted views.* In: Early Childhood Education: Issues and Developments. New York: Nova Science Publishers.

Boucher, J. (2017). *Autism spectrum disorders: Characteristics, causes and practical issues.* SAGE Publications.

Brigham, T. J. (2015). An introduction to gamification: Adding game elements for engagement. *Medical Reference Services Quarterly, 34*(4), 471-480. https://doi.org/10.1080/02763869.2015.1082385

Campisi, L., Imran, N., Nazeer, A., Skokauskas, N., & Azeem, M. W. (2018). Autism spectrum disorder. *British Medical Bulletin, 127*(1), 91-100. https://doi: 10.1093/bmb/ldy026

Courchesne, V., Langlois, V., Gregoire, P., St-Denis, A., Bouvet, L., Ostrolenk, A. & Mottron, L. (2020). Interests and strengths in autism, useful but misunderstood: A pragmatic case-study. *Frontiers in Psychology, 11*(569339), 1-13. https://doi.org/10.3389/fpsyg.2020.569339

Dunst, C. J., Trivette, C. M. & Masiello, T. (2010). Influence of the interests of children with autism on everyday learning opportunities. *Psychological Reports, 107*(1), 281-288. https://doi.org/10.2466/04.10.11.15.21.PR0.107.4.281-288

Frederickson, N. & Cline, T. (2015). *Special educational needs, inclusion and diversity.* Maidenhead: McGraw-Hill Education.

Gunn, K. C. M. & Delafield-Butt, J. T. (2016). Teaching children with autism spectrum disorder with restricted interests: A review of evidence for best practice. *Review of Educational Research, 86*(2), 408–430. https://doi.org/10.3102/0034654315604027

Harackiewicz, J. M., Smith, J. L. & Priniski, S. J. (2016). Interest matters: The importance of promoting interest in education. *Policy Insights from the*

Behavioral and Brain Sciences, 3(2), 220-227. https://doi.org/10.1177/237273
2216655542

Hodges, H., Fealko, C. & Soares, N. (2020). Autism spectrum disorder: Definition,
epidemiology, causes, and clinical evaluation. *TP Translational Pediatrics, 9*(1),
55-65. https://doi.org/10.21037%2Ftp.2019.09.09

Kim, S., Song, K., Lockee, B., & Burton, J. (2017). What is gamification in learning
and education?. In *Gamification in Learning and Education. Advances in
Game-Based Learning.* Springer, Cham. https://doi.org/10.1007/978-3-319-
47283-6_4

Klin, A., Saulnier, C. A., Sparrow, S. S., Cicchetti, D. V., Volkmar, F. R. & Lord, C.
(2007). Social and communication abilities and disabilities in higher functioning
individuals with autism spectrum disorders: The Vineland and the ADOS.
Journal of Autism and Developmental Disorders, 37(4), 748-759. https://doi.o
rg/10.1007/s10803-006-0229-4

Kodak, T., Cariveau, T., LeBlanc, B. A., Mahon, J. J. & Carroll, R. A. (2017).
Selection and implementation of skill acquisition programs by special
education teachers and staff for students with autism spectrum disorder.
Behavior Modification, 41(1), 58-83. https://doi.org/10.1177/0145445517692081

Kolb, D. (1984). *Experiential learning: Experience as the source of learning and
development.* prentice hall.

National Autistic Society. (2020). *What is autism?* https://www.autism.org.uk
/advice-and-guidance/what-is-autism.

Odom, S. L., Collet-Klingenberg, L., Rogers, S. J. & Hatton, D. D. (2010).
Evidence-based practices in interventions for children and youth with autism
spectrum disorders. *Preventing School Failure: Alternative Education for
Children and Youth, 54*(4), 275-282. https://doi.org/10.1080/10459881003785506

Paudel, P. (2021). Online education: Benefits, challenges and strategies during
and after COVID-19 in higher education. *International Journal on Studies in
Education (IJonSE), 3*(2), 70-85. https://doi.org/10.46328/ijonse.32

Ruble, L. A., & Robson, D. M. (2007). Individual and environmental determinants
of engagement in autism. *Journal of Autism and Developmental Disorders,
37*(8), 1457–1468. https://doi.org/10.1007/s10803-006-0222-y

Rutkin, A. (2016). *How Minecraft is helping children with autism make new
friends.* New Scientist. Available at: https://www.newscientist.com/article/mg
23030713-100-how-is-helping-children-with-autism-make-new-friends.

Wearmouth, J. (2017). *Special educational needs and disabilities in schools: A
critical introduction.* Bloomsbury Academic.

Wearmouth, J. & Butler, C. (2020). Special educational needs co-ordinators'
perceptions of effective provision for including autistic children in primary
and middle schools in England. *Education 3-13, 4*(3), 258-272. https://doi.org
/10.1080/03004279.2019.1664401

Chapter 4

To a Wide Audience: Writing in Multiple Modes and Genres

Anastasia R. Wickham

Reach University

Abstract: Wickham looks at middle school writing projects and how adding a multi-genre approach to teaching can help students build better projects.

Keywords: Middle school; multi-genre; writing projects

***

Remember life before smartphones and tablets connected via ubiquitous Wi-Fi? Thinking back to life before constant connection might be hard for us as adults but is impossible for adolescents who never knew that world. Yet, if you walked into many classrooms today, you might be struck by how little instructional approaches have changed. Although exponential technological innovations have changed our society in profound ways in the last 15 years, institutions like schools are not built to redirect quickly. Educators must follow synchronized curriculum requirements to guide instruction, and the process of crafting, vetting, and adopting these standards takes time. To put the varying rates of change into perspective, the Common Core standards implemented by most states in the U.S. were released in 2010. That was the same year the first iPad was sold. Since then, the world has exploded with interactive and accessible content that is delivered in entertaining ways. In some classroom contexts, though, the lecture is still employed in English/Language Arts (ELA) classrooms with the end goal of students producing essays like those we wrote in school before digital tools transformed the concept of research and the ways in which we share information.

Like teachers in every discipline, ELA teachers must now reevaluate the skills, knowledge, and dispositions that students will need to be successful in a digitally connected world, not only as employees but as people. To what extent technological advances have fundamentally changed us is up for debate, as is whether the changes are beneficial or harmful. What seems clear, though, is that teachers now vie for students' attention amid highly elevated sensory input provided by the technological devices we use daily. Curricular and pedagogical innovations seem inevitable if educators aim to engage students while exposing them to and preparing them for current realities.

Still, to assume that a lack of pedagogical change is problematic and therefore revamp curricula without careful examination is not the answer. Allowing technology to drive instruction creates its own problems. The key is to hold onto what works in the classroom while mindfully incorporating new tools–not an easy task. Technological advances necessarily must change some of the ways in which we approach preparing adolescents for adult life, but certainly, we cannot predict all the ways in which technology will shape our future society. Change simply happens too quickly. For instructional standards and methods to hold up, they must be written with room for pedagogical interpretation and adaptation.

This year, for example, ChatGPT, "OpenAI's text-generating AI chatbot," captured the attention of educators around the world (Stringer & Wiggers, 2023). From dire predictions that education would never survive AI-based writing tools to exuberance over new possibilities, reactions have varied significantly. While the technology is new, the response is not. Changes that come with such advanced tools *should* give us pause. The implications are vast and are yet unknown. Still, ignoring the tools is not a viable path. In the context of writing instruction, the tricky balance is to embrace what technological tools can provide without viewing them as a replacement for qualified teachers and sound instructional strategies. Instead, resources like ChatGPT should prompt teachers to think deeply about what we teach students, why we prioritize that knowledge, and the role that AI tools can play in meeting educational objectives. Without effective teachers to translate curricular requirements into lessons that work in their evolving contexts, the requirements mean little.

The best teachers cannot rely on static curricula because they know that students' needs, interests, and motivations change, just as the world around us evolves. These dynamic educators combine the art and science of teaching to create standards-based lessons that are engaging and relevant. Kalantzis and Cope (2023) point out that even people who have a "natural knack" for teaching benefit from the science of education. Resources like the Universal Design for Learning (UDL) framework furnish guidelines that supply educators with a format for implementing that science to design a curriculum that will address learning goals while challenging and engaging all learners (Cast, 2023). Using the UDL guidelines encourages teachers to examine the how, what, and why of learning. Likewise, when it comes to writing instruction in the age of AI tools like

ChatGPT, the first step is to assess what it is that we really want our students to know and be able to do. After that, we can decide how best to achieve that outcome.

What are we humans uniquely suited to write? In what ways can writing fulfill and educate us? Essential questions like these can center our intentions. By exploring and continually evaluating the answers, a lens through which to view pedagogical choices emerges. Kalantzis and Cope (2023) provide three questions for the reform of literacy that are useful in this work:

1. Why? What's happening in the world that requires to change in the frame of reference for literacy?
2. What? Then what should we be teaching in a reformed program for literacy?
3. How? And what is an appropriate pedagogy?

This work on multiliteracies offers a roadmap to the kinds of transformation we can embrace to make our classrooms more relevant. After exploring these questions comes the work of fulfilling the demands dictated by curriculum requirements in new ways.

As an example, the seventh-grade Common Core standards can be used to illustrate how foundational knowledge and skills can be acquired using technologies and media that did not exist at their inception. This expansion serves to motivate students while ensuring a level of technological equity. Multigenre, multimodal exposure, and opportunities for composition provide students with choices that allow for relevance to their lives while honoring their unique voices and empowering them to decide what knowledge to share and how to share it.

Why Multigenre Research Papers?

How exactly are technological advances related to writing assignments? To begin, the types of writing our students see and need to master are changing exponentially. Think about our consumption of the news as an example of the changing world of text. Where newspapers in generations past had little color and few pictures, digital news stories today regularly include multiple modes. In fact, interaction with the internet has normalized multimodal text to the point that we can forget that we are even interacting with multiple modes. For example, a news article with embedded photos, audio, and video clips is no longer noteworthy. The children in schools today have grown up in a multimodal environment. Online writing models break up long blocks of text with other modes of content delivery. Additionally, technology can impact student writing via instructional methods, but more about that aspect later.

Imagine sitting down to grade student work and encountering a humorous take on an ode to gluten followed by a short film starring digitally rendered Tardigrades (water bears) as superheroes. Both are components of projects I have received over the years. The first was authored by a student who had recently been diagnosed with Celiac Disease. She wanted to learn all she could about the diagnosis while finding a way to cope with the loss of some of her favorite foods. The latter was composed by a student who was fascinated by water bears and wanted to find a metaphorical way to illustrate their ability to withstand extreme conditions that would kill other species.

Writing teachers know that the wrong assignment prompt can lead to hours of grading uninspired papers that are as tedious to read as they probably were to write. Multigenre Research Papers (MGRPs) provide a structured yet open way to incorporate variety in the composition process. With MGRPs, teachers can facilitate the attainment of research skills while teaching multiple genres. Generally, students choose a topic they care about, such as the examples above, which boosts their motivation and passion for the project. Once they land on a topic, students research with the purpose of learning enough to compose a compelling paper. As the project progresses, students also make creative choices about which genre and mode to use to share information about their subject. To make informed choices, they have to learn about various types of writing and the questions that drive the choices, such as:

1.   Who is the audience?
2.   What is my purpose (to inform, persuade, entertain, explore, etc.)?
3.   Which mode(s) best fulfill my purpose given the target audience?

Having a research project that students value anchors the lessons on writing; students can apply what they learn about a new genre or mode right away instead of learning for a possible future assignment.

Since the 1990s, Multigenre Research Papers (MGRPs) have been widely adopted and adapted. Much credit for sparking the initial conversation belongs to Tom Romano, Professor Emeritus at Miami University, and long-time writing instructor. His 1995 book, *Writing with Passion: Life Stories, Multiple Genres* began the exploration of combining genres with a central focus on allowing and encouraging students to write about topics for which they have enthusiasm and attachment. Whether it be intellectual or emotional, Romano argues that writing comes to life when imbued with passion[1]. Later, in 2000, Romano's *Blending Genre, Altering Style: Writing Multigenre Research Papers* was published

---

[1] See Romano's (2023) recent poem, "The Truth about Why I Love Teaching," in Appendix A.

and further developed the concept of using MGRPs in the classroom by providing practical advice, teaching tips, and student samples.

Some of the beauty of the MGRP lies in its flexibility. Just as students are invited to make choices, teachers shape the assignment to align with the grade level and general topic they wish to cover, as well as the desired learning outcomes. While students *will* learn about the topic they research, the purpose is often to attain transferable writing and research skills, along with an appreciation for the writing process, over specific content knowledge. Writing to learn content is a valid exercise, but the goal here is primarily to be able to research and write for varied audiences, contexts, and purposes. A decade later, the student who wrote "An Ode to Gluten," may not remember all the facts about the structural protein, but she may remember that an ode is written to praise something. She might even remember the general style and format of this type of poetry. Perhaps most importantly, she might remember how the act of putting words together and sharing them with others carried her through a difficult time, and how she had moments of laughter even when the world looked dark. In some cases, the emphasis is on skills over knowledge–what students can do with the information they retrieve. Sometimes the important lesson lies in the human capacity to feel and share emotional responses via text. Distinguishing which lessons we want students to take away from our classes matters, as does listening carefully to the lessons students value.

Another way that teachers can tailor the MGRP assignment to their classes is by choosing the number and type of genres students may incorporate. As an example, we will focus on a seventh-grade ELA class. Using the Common Core state standards as a guide, we can plan the assignment in such a way that virtually all standards are addressed as students work through the required genres. Figure 4.1 illustrates a sample alignment of the genre with grade-level CCSS reading and writing objectives. A reflection on the MGRP writing process is always included in the project, as well. While this alignment is specific, I have used MGRPs across multiple grade levels and with varied curricular requirements.

Figure 4.1. Sample Chart: Genres and 7th Grade Common Core State Standards

Genre	CCSS Focal Area	
Narrative	Reading Literature	Writing Narratives
News story	Reading Informational Texts	Writing Informative Texts
Essay	Reading Informational Texts	Writing Arguments
Poetry	Reading Literature	Discipline-Specific Writing

Each component of the MGRP is introduced in class using various modes as models. Once the concept is grasped, students move on to "read" additional models to gain a sense of the genre. Through this exercise, students cover the reading standards and prepare to write their own examples. By the end, students will understand how genre and mode affect writing. Once this awareness has been achieved, students have the tools to choose and implement an appropriate genre for a given writing task. While this chart focuses on employing the assignment to meet the needs of a seventh-grade class using specific standards, the ease with which the MGRP has been shaped to fulfill varied objectives is a testament to its flexibility.

Another layer of the MGRP project is the research. Synthesizing research into a product that is multigenre arguably requires a deeper level of understanding of the subject. Thinking back to the essential questions on what motivates us to write, we know that choice and freedom have an impact. With MGRPs, authors can choose a subject about which they are passionate and lean into genres that display their strengths. A level of differentiation is baked in. What ELA teachers perhaps fear most with the rise of services like ChatGPT is that students will lose the ability to think for themselves and articulate their thoughts in meaningful ways. In the end, the paper is not likely to be something that could be quickly created by AI tools, but what matters more is why this is true. While each piece conceivably could be written by a program like ChatGPT, students would still need to gain some level of knowledge of the subject and make compositional choices to successfully achieve their desired outcomes.

For example, a high school student once wrote about true crimes that had been committed in the state in which I taught. One of the student's MGRP entries was a news interview with a fictional neighbor after a crime had been committed. Another entry was a posthumous journal entry by one of the survivors. Even at its current level of operation, ChatGPT can create excerpts such as these; however, the creativity the student displayed in making those compositional choices was valuable. Ultimately, educators will always face complex choices regarding the placement of technology and the effort we expend to uphold academic integrity in a changing world.

Beyond the aforementioned advantages of MGRP assignments, students encounter compelling examples of the genres and modes they write in the world around them, unlike the traditional five-paragraph essay, which seems relegated only to the classroom and divorced from real life. Relevant assignments that incorporate components of choice and authentic student voice not only empower students but also allow for *enjoyment* during the research and writing process.

Multimedia Instructional Models

While working as a middle school reading specialist, I realized that the students who needed the most support with foundational reading skills like decoding needed to simultaneously learn grade-level ELA concepts like the elements of plot and characterization. Using only stories from the textbook, we lacked a quick way to get everyone on the same page so we could practice new skills. While leveled texts worked well to differentiate nonfiction reading without students losing relevant facts, evocative fiction is about more than relaying information. Originally, we used familiar fairy tales and children's books, but I wanted more novelty, along with nuance and complexity, without textual barriers. The solution: film shorts. Disney shorts, like "La Luna," for example, craft highly engaging stories bundled into tiny packages. "La Luna" runs just under seven minutes long, but includes a plot, three characters, a moral, and themes of tradition and innovation. Another bonus is that "La Luna," like many other short films, does not rely on spoken language (the characters communicate in gibberish), so language learners are not at a disadvantage.

Lest you imagine that this is a dumbing down of pedagogy, the tactic of implementing video for instructional purposes is also used by professors of law, like George Fisher (2018) at Stanford, who notes that "video clips don't divide the class into leaders and laggards, those prepared for class and those not. Everyone sees the clip together" (p. 15). The focus, therefore, shifts to the skill, whether it be arguing a case or outlining a plot. In the case of the MGRP project, films can be used to teach the elements of a story that students will need when they begin to create their own stories. The motivation to learn comes not only from engaging instruction but from the knowledge that the students will be applying what they have learned to write their own stories. The knowledge is not theoretical, nor is it memorized for a test. Instead, students are already in the process of shaping their own multigenre papers when they begin to learn about additional genres that they can incorporate. An effective way to help students transfer knowledge and skills is to provide a template for students to practice analyzing plot and characterization that can then be used to plan their own stories.

Fictionalized news stories built around facts are another potential component of the MGRP. Often students choose a well-known figure as the topic, so imagine interviews with Billie Holiday, for example. Creative exercises in which students must develop a knowledge base on a topic and then use that information to imagine responses in unknown contexts build critical thinking skills and the kind of writing skills that authors use to bring characters to life. We can see these skills in popular audio mediums like narrative nonfiction podcasts. Even when conducting interviews, podcasters have to make choices about what information to include, what questions to ask, and how to most effectively build the story.

Using video and audio interviews as a teaching tool centers discussions on these rhetorical choices while serving as examples for the genre and mode. Once students know how an interview would be formatted, they can choose to present it as a written transcript, as part of a news story, or as an audio clip, to name a few options.

Often students are drawn to a topic because it represents something larger that is important for the student. For example, the student who chose Billie Holiday wanted to explore not only the specifics of the singer's life but also the historical and present ways in which race and gender shape our lives. She wanted to tell Holiday's story as part of a larger story. Choong and Bjork (2023) highlight this aspect of the interview, writing: "Through sharing the stories of their interview subjects, students learn to walk the line between honoring the particularities of their interviewees' experiences and talking about those experiences within broader social contexts" (p. 555). Allowing students to tell stories that matter to them in ways that they have chosen empowers them, not only to create but to share what they have created. In sharing her project on Billie Holiday, this student brought awareness to issues that were new for some students. When she had another student come to the front to share a dual-voice presentation of the interview she had created with Holiday, the class leaned forward. There was emotion and a sense that Billie Holiday had been a real person, just like all of us. By connecting with a voice and demonstrating how that one voice connects to others, we have the "potential to work toward social change" (Choong & Bjork, 2023, p. 551).

Beyond narrative nonfiction, interviews, news stories, and other short stories, MGRP projects often include poetry. Poetry in the classroom is tricky. While I contend that most students really do like poetry once they have been exposed to enough of it, they often resist, at least initially. Nothing evokes classroom groans quite like the mention of poetry. This fact is baffling when we consider the emotion and passion that fill the adolescent years. Perhaps what students dislike is not poetry, but the antiquated brand of poetry we often read in school, poetry that feels disconnected from the students' lives.

Remember that the purpose of assigning the MGRP and teaching the components with multimodal tools is to imbue the space with engagement and relevance. The right poetry can do the same, but as Vázquez (2023) points out, "Young people need spaces where they can practice the magic of poetry for themselves" (p. 53). As they practice, though, they need models. Spaces like YouTube allow teachers to bring into the classroom the voices and visuals of poets with messages that resonate with our students.

Hearing other young people proudly share their spoken art opens doors. One example is fourteen-year-old Brandon Sanders and twelve-year-old Mikeala Miller, who performed original poems at the "If You Give a Child a Word" TEDx event in Fort Worth, Texas. They share, together and individually, inspiring poems about their lives, their hopes, and their visions for the future, each beginning with one word that was meaningful to them. After watching the performances, middle school students might play with poetry by choosing a single word to embody the topic of their MGRP. Maybe Billie Holiday's word would be "innovation," while another student writes a comical "Ode to Gluten." Whatever the topic, poetry creates a space for wordplay. The poems can be touching, inspiring, funny, or dark, the full range of emotions that adolescents grapple with. As Vázquez (2023) writes, "Poetry has a unique capacity for enabling us to bear the vicissitudes of human existence" (p. 55). Autobiographical writing certainly has a place in the classroom, but exploring another's emotions can build empathy and mitigate our own feelings of isolation. Poems, according to Vázquez, "bring the English language alive for young people, touching on themes at once local and universal" (p. 52). At the heart of our work, we teach English to provide students with experiences like this.

Student Choice, Student Voice

Recently, in *English Education*, Mary L. Neville (2023), an assistant professor of K-12 literacy education in the School of Teacher Preparation, Administration, and Leadership at New Mexico State University wrote: "Teachers and students need the fullness of their literacies reflected in the ELA classroom" (p. 95). In her article, "Noticing Texts as Equity-Oriented English Education," she points out the choice involved in what we notice, both as teachers and students, explaining: "There is a choice in our noticing. We have a choice to center those texts we and our students love, to highlight joy or to uncover injustice, to be moved by a play on words or an image of a Pokémon metaphor" (Neville, 2023, p. 111). As teachers, we signal to students what kinds of text matter, explicitly and implicitly. While organizations like the International Literacy Association (ILA), the National Council of Teachers of English (NCTE), and the Assembly on Literature for Adolescents of NCTE (ALAN) have long provided evidence that offering students a choice in what they read leads to better outcomes, it is important to remember that students are not always aware of the choices that exist unless teachers introduce them. Unfortunately, not all students grow up in text-rich environments. On the other hand, some students forgo their preferred choices because they have not seen similar texts in the classroom and therefore assume they are not valid academic choices. Neville addresses such omissions when she calls for all literacies to be reflected in our classrooms. For choice to be most valuable and genuine, students need to understand what choices exist and feel validated in making the choices that call to them. The MGRP facilitates this process by covering mini-lessons on multiple modes and genres and by providing a multitude of models that illustrate the vast world of textual possibilities.

As teachers, we know that no two students are alike. We all have unique gifts and past experiences to bring into the classroom, but too often students are asked to check those identities at the door. But we can approach writing instruction differently. As Turner et al. (2023) point out: "Multimodality also invites you to come as you are . . . you're coming as you are, and you're using the things that you see around you every day to communicate your message" (p. 299). When we as teachers open our eyes to the kinds of text creation and consumption our students are already engaged in, we unlock the gate to relevance and invite engagement. We also create a space in which we are not always the knowledgeable sage; students may be the experts, especially when it comes to new technologies, and they are often eager to share their knowledge if they see that we are genuinely interested.

Giving students a voice, especially those students who have felt marginalized in the school setting, is powerful. The process takes time and patience, as students unlearn past expectations. An MGRP assignment invites students to make choices and to write about topics they care about in ways that make sense to them, but for some students, this can feel unsettling. Even teachers and students can co-create the expectations of the project, but first, we must create relationships that allow for this kind of exchange. In "Writing Beyond Borders: Latinx Voices in World Literature," Holly Spinelli (2023) addresses her experience with creating this kind of classroom community, writing, "Slowly, the students began to build trust with one another and with me. Their voices filled a majority of our space. They began creating the course content and focus" (p. 82). When students witness our sincere commitment to honoring their voices, classroom spaces transform.

Reading and writing are two sides of the same coin, so reading choice and student voice are interrelated. By welcoming diverse authors' voices, we invite students to explore their own literacy more fully. In "Crossing into New Sanctuaries: Poetic Pedagogy for the Often Unseen," Esteban Rodríguez (2023) reflects on the power teachers have to change the landscape of the English/Language Arts classroom by allowing students to focus on reading and writing projects that speak to them. The case he highlights details a student's reluctance to engage with novels, but his connection to poetry. Speaking of a Spanish/English bilingual student he calls David, he says:

> There is no ideal world, however, and while I found that many students connected with the substance of what I taught, there were just as many who did not. David did not connect with the novels. While I could give him failing scores for the assignments related to those novels, called his

mother and told her that her son was not meeting expectations, or simply ignored him and let him become someone who did less than the bare minimum, I did not. I wanted David to choose what he wanted to learn, and he wanted to learn poetry. (Rodriguez, 2023, p. 31).

Similarly, Spinelli (2023) finds that the composition process becomes relevant to a wider range of students when they have not only reading choices but also input in the products they compose. She writes that some students "wanted a hands-on research project option. These students opted to create drawings, paintings, collages, music videos, and traditional foods to share the histories, cultures, and experiences of their own cultures across the world" (Spinelli, 2023, p. 86).

Park (2023) discusses the ways in which first-generation college students develop their identities as writers, and one way to encourage this development is to encourage a "[m]ultivocal approach" that fuses the multiple discourses that are part of a student's life p. 242). With MGRPs, the ability to code switch, incorporating multiple modes, genres, and discourses is a strength, not a deficit. Students are given more control over their final product, using what Williamson (2023) calls "managed nonmanagement," which refers to "intentionally reserving space for students to exist as writers free from direct managerial control" (p. 284). Nowell and Smith (2023) reinforce the value of a student-directed approach, writing:

We hope that teachers and leaders of all kinds can recognize the value of creating culturally sustaining units, outside of data and skills. Our students got to read, write, and talk about issues and people that were relevant and actually mattered to them. They got to see their own cultures as worthy of study in the ELA classroom. (p. 49)

Providing a diverse, text-rich classroom in which students ultimately have choices means moving beyond the occasional inclusion of relevant and culturally varied messages and media. This commitment requires teachers to give up some curricular control by focusing on the essential knowledge, skills, and dispositions they want to cultivate. Further, this work can only be achieved when students feel empowered enough to share honest reflections. As Williamson (2023) reminds us, "it is not necessarily the presence of a particular practice in the classroom that transforms work... Any strategy can become industrialized, and therefore distant from students, despite teachers' good intentions" (p. 288). This transformational work takes ongoing care.

Empowerment: Composition as Activism

One of the essential dispositions that teachers want to instill in students is the valuing of the writing process. We discuss creating lifelong readers more often, but lifelong writers possess a practice that can be used for personal fulfillment, clear thinking, reflection, and so much more than the obvious and necessary career purposes. A step in the right direction is to allow students to see themselves as writers. In addition to removing cultural biases about what texts matter, showcasing a variety of modes and genres allows the class to focus on the questions that all writers need to answer. Teachers can nudge students toward an understanding of rhetorical choices, leading discussions on audience awareness, the purpose of a text, and even who has access to that text and who is left out. This kind of cultural competency is highlighted in Butler and Bick's (2023) "Audience Awareness and Access: The Design of Sound and Captions as Valuable Composition Practices," in which they forefront questions of access in classroom analysis, writing, "The connection between *audience awareness* and *access* . . . allows us to elevate the field's growing recognition of the essential role of designing access in multimodal composition processes" (p. 418). The inherently multimodal nature of captioning sound is fertile ground on which to grow students' understanding of how written text can best express sound to provide access to a broader audience. Intriguing questions about what is lost in translation and what extra layers of meaning can be conveyed in either mode arise when doing this work, questions that allow students to see themselves as writers making choices that matter. In Butler and Bick's study, they note: "Along with students creating videos, podcasts, and other projects, teacher-scholars continue to reveal new possibilities for composition as the process in which designers orchestrate multiple modes of meaning" (p. 420).

Expanding discussions of audience awareness to include multiple modes and questions of (dis)abilities provides the backdrop students need to see why and how these choices matter. Butler and Bick (2023) offer criteria and questions for assessing access and audience awareness in multimodal composition processes, two of which adapt well to an MGRP project:

1. Multiple modes of access: Does the composition provide access through multiple modes? For example, does the composition provide visual access to sound as well as aural access to visuals?

2. Multimodal Communication: Does the composition communicate meaning through multiple modes in order to reach different audiences? For example, does the composition communicate meaning through visuals and sound? (p. 420)

While the class in Butler and Bick's (2023) study debriefed after working with video subtitles, they expressed what the extra layer of text added for everyone, not only the original focus audience of people experiencing hearing loss. Imagine the power of students making these discoveries through their own work instead of simply copying the takeaway from a class slide deck.

Enjoyment: Creating Lifelong Writers

For those of us who continue to write after we have left our final ELA classroom, why do we persist? The answers help us grow a new generation of writers. A compelling reason for writing is connection. Even when we journal, laying down words for only ourselves, we develop a deeper connection with our own hearts and minds. Arguably, though, this connection is lost in many classrooms. With the pressures of curriculum requirements and testing, not to mention the myriad of other distractions that teachers encounter every day, we can forget the real reasons people write. Williamson (2023) reminds us to consider continually how we use our classroom writing space, adding, "Working conditions for students and teachers in literacy classrooms are often dehumanizing, concerned more with business and efficiency than meaning or human connection" (p. 289). Not everything meaningful can be easily measured. The human connection created when a student shares her MGRP, a multimodal, multigenre product of her creation, defies quantification. The value outweighs the score on the rubric.

In addition to the power of human connection to instill a love of writing, teachers must attend to the development of students' writer identities. People rarely enjoy tasks for which they feel ill-suited. When we foster a sense of belonging and prepare students to undertake writing tasks with the belief that they can grow and improve, we up the odds that they will see themselves as writers. Inventing and affirming writer identities is especially important for students who enter the classroom space lacking a sense of belonging. Jie Y. Park (2023) of Clark University addresses this concern in "Agency, Identity, and Writing: Perspectives from First-Generation Students of Color in Their First Year of College." Park's study "suggests the value of classroom activities and interactions that develop students' awareness of self and writing, and self *in* writing" (p. 244). While the focus is on college students, the questions posed by Park apply to all writers who find themselves at odds with the writing we traditionally expect at school:

1. What makes academic writing "academic"?
2. What is the relationship between reading and writing academic texts?
3. What are some differences in writing across academic disciplines?
4. Who is my audience? What role does the audience play in how I write?
5. What are some of the resources–social, cultural, academic–that I bring? (p. 233)

The MGRP invites students to break the rules of "academic" writing when it makes sense to do so, just as authors of all genres defy reader expectations in effective ways. The assignment brings to life explorations of audience and conventions based on genre and mode. Perhaps most importantly, the project invites and celebrates social, cultural, and linguistic diversity.

The National Council of Teachers of English (NCTE, 2022) "advocates for writing instruction that builds on students' strengths, that values their many ways of using language, that promotes a broad view of what constitutes 'text,' and that promotes young people's voices and purposes for writing within authentic contexts." For teachers striving to provide enough space to broaden the definitions of "text" while inviting students to use their authentic voices, the MGRP provides an efficient way to incorporate new genres, modes, and codes. Moving beyond linguistic code-switching to include visual expression, for example, makes sense in a world where the visual and verbal coincide. According to Turner et al. (2023), this expansion overcomes a racial bias, as well; they assert that "[c]reativity is especially important when you're talking about racial justice because our visual and multimodal creativities, as people of color, are rarely acknowledged and valued by societal systems and spaces" (p. 299).

Conclusion

How can ELA teachers follow NCTE's guidelines to honor all students' language while adhering to standards and preparing students for their writing futures? Centering student choice and student voice is a powerful start. Student empowerment is also essential, and we can empower students when we show them ways to expand their literacies and when they see themselves as writers in a broad sense. Finally, students' writing improves when they practice. This piece requires classroom time and space but is most effective when students enjoy writing enough to practice outside of the classroom, as well. Enjoyment is amplified when lessons are relevant and delivered using engaging methods. To pretend that MGRP projects come together seamlessly and reach all students is misleading. Writing is complex and teaching is difficult; pairing the two is a tall order. However, while Neville (2023) acknowledges that teachers have overwhelming demands, she writes: "Even in the midst of the many challenges to responsive writing curriculum, equity-oriented English educators have offered ways to support students in seeing themselves as full writers and taking joy in their multiple, historicized, and future-oriented literacies" (p. 77). Multigenre research papers invite students to step into the role of writer, making complex decisions about how to present material. As they work through the process, we can remind them to reflect on the essential questions that remain at the heart of composition, even as the world changes: What are we humans uniquely suited to write? In what ways can writing fulfill and educate us?

Appendix A: "The Truth about Why I Love to Teach Writing"

(after Mekeel McBride's poem "The Truth about Why I Love Potatoes")

1

Of everything you experience in school, learning to write
might be the most magical: You have an itch and grab
language, translate it into symbols on napkin, notebook,
yellow pad, screen. With nothing said aloud, meaning
blooms in readers' minds.

2

I guess I forgot to mention how writing can heal your hurt,
spread balm on regrets. You start with what you remember,
an image, a smell, a fragment of language. You write what
you don't expect. If you stay honest and press with detail,
words hold their breath and dive to depths you've never
been. They bring understanding to the surface.

3

If writing were a person, it would be a gardener. It would
step into the cold greenhouse in March, turn on the space
heater to boost the day's dim sunshine. Like a gardener
sowing seeds, writing in profligate, pushing words just deep
enough into a draft to sprout. When ideas shoulder through
to light, a gardener is gentle, attentive, encouraging with
water and nutrients. When plants are strong, she is ruthless,
selecting, thinning, repotting. A gardener trusts process.
Growth and development are her watchwords.

4

Teachers who write know there is surprising language and
perception dormant in the most unpromising students.

5

If I could have my wish, every teacher would teach writing.
It's the essential skill to nurture in all students. They learn

faith in the language in them, fearlessness heading down the
page with it. They learn the pleasure of finding the right
words, of treasuring linguistic rhythms, of shaping evolving
meaning. As they write to find truth in essays, stories, and
poems, they become better readers, too.

–Tom Romano, 2023

Appendix B: Standards Alignment

Table 4.1. American 7th grade standards for reading and writing

MGRP Component	7th Grade English Language Arts Common Core State Standards: Reading		7th Grade English Language Arts Common Core State Standards: Writing	
Narrative	R.L.7.1	Cite several pieces of textual evidence to support analysis of what the text says explicitly as well as inferences drawn from the text.	W.7.3.A	Engage and orient the reader by establishing a context and point of view and introducing a narrator and/or characters; organize an event sequence that unfolds naturally and logically.
	R.L.7.2	Determine a theme or central idea of a text and analyze its development over the course of the text; provide an objective summary of the text.	W.7.3.B	Use narrative techniques, such as dialogue, pacing, and description, to develop experiences, events, and/or characters.
	R.L.7.3	Analyze how particular elements of a story or drama interact (e.g., how setting shapes the characters or plot).	W.7.3.C	Use a variety of transition words, phrases, and clauses to convey sequence and signal shifts from one time frame or setting to another.
	R.L.7.6	Analyze how an author develops and contrasts the points of view of different characters or narrators in a text.	W.7.3.D	Use precise words and phrases, relevant descriptive details, and sensory language to capture the action and convey experiences and events.
	R.L.7.9	Compare and contrast a fictional portrayal of a time, place, or character and a historical account of the same period as a means of understanding how	W.7.3.E	Provide a conclusion that follows from and reflects on the narrated experiences or events.

MGRP Component	7th Grade English Language Arts Common Core State Standards: Reading		7th Grade English Language Arts Common Core State Standards: Writing	
		authors of fiction use or alter history.		
	R.L.7.10	By the end of the year, read and comprehend literature, including stories, dramas, and poems, in the grades 6–8 text complexity band proficiently, with scaffolding as needed at the high end of the range.	W.7.9.A	Apply grade 7 Reading standards to literature (e.g., "Compare and contrast a fictional portrayal of a time, place, or character and a historical account of the same period as a means of understanding how authors of fiction use or alter history").
News	R.I.7.1	Cite several pieces of textual evidence to support analysis of what the text says explicitly as well as inferences drawn from the text.	W.7.1.A	Introduce claim(s), acknowledge alternate or opposing claims, and organize the reasons and evidence logically.
	R.I.7.2	Determine two or more central ideas in a text and analyze their development over the course of the text; provide an objective summary of the text.	W.7.1.B	Support claim(s) with logical reasoning and relevant evidence, using accurate, credible sources and demonstrating an understanding of the topic or text.
	R.I.7.3	Analyze the interactions between individuals, events, and ideas in a text (e.g., how ideas influence individuals or events, or how individuals influence ideas or events).	W.7.1.C	Use words, phrases, and clauses to create cohesion and clarify the relationships among claim(s), reasons, and evidence.

MGRP Component	7th Grade English Language Arts Common Core State Standards: Reading		7th Grade English Language Arts Common Core State Standards: Writing	
	R.I.7.5	Analyze the structure an author uses to organize a text, including how the major sections contribute to the whole and to the development of the ideas.	W.7.1.D	Establish and maintain a formal style.
	R.I.7.8	Trace and evaluate the argument and specific claims in a text, assessing whether the reasoning is sound and the evidence is relevant and sufficient to support the claims.	W.7.I.E	Provide a concluding statement or section that follows from and supports the argument presented.
	R.I.7.10	By the end of the year, read and comprehend literary nonfiction in the grades 6–8 text complexity band proficiently, with scaffolding as needed at the high end of the range.	W.7.2.A	Introduce a topic clearly, previewing what is to follow; organize ideas, concepts, and information, using strategies such as definition, classification, comparison/contrast, and cause/ effect; include formatting (e.g., headings), graphics (e.g., charts, tables), and multimedia when useful to aiding comprehension.
			W.7.9.B	Apply grade 7 Reading standards to literary nonfiction (e.g. "Trace and evaluate the argument and specific claims in a text, assessing whether the reasoning is sound and the evidence

MGRP Component	7th Grade English Language Arts Common Core State Standards: Reading		7th Grade English Language Arts Common Core State Standards: Writing	
				is relevant and sufficient to support the claims").
Interview	RL.7.1	Cite several pieces of textual evidence to support analysis of what the text says explicitly as well as inferences drawn from the text.	W.7.2.A	Introduce a topic clearly, previewing what is to follow; organize ideas, concepts, and information, using strategies such as definition, classification, comparison/contrast, and cause/ effect; include formatting (e.g., headings), graphics (e.g., charts, tables), and multimedia when useful to aiding comprehension.
	R.I.7.4	Determine the meaning of words and phrases as they are used in a text, including figurative, connotative, and technical meanings; analyze the impact of a specific word choice on meaning and tone.	W.7.2.B	Develop the topic with relevant facts, definitions, concrete details, quotations, or other information and examples.
	R.I.7.6	Determine an author's point of view or purpose in a text and analyze how the author distinguishes his or her position from that of others.	W.7.2.C	Use appropriate transitions to create cohesion and clarify the relationships among ideas and concepts.
	R.I.7.10	By the end of the year, read and comprehend literary nonfiction in the grades 6–8 text complexity band proficiently, with	W.7.2.D	Use precise language and domain-specific vocabulary to inform about or explain the topic.

MGRP Component	7th Grade English Language Arts Common Core State Standards: Reading		7th Grade English Language Arts Common Core State Standards: Writing	
		scaffolding as needed at the high end of the range.		
			W.7.9.B	Apply grade 7 Reading standards to literary nonfiction (e.g. "Trace and evaluate the argument and specific claims in a text, assessing whether the reasoning is sound and the evidence is relevant and sufficient to support the claims").
Interview	RL.7.1	Cite several pieces of textual evidence to support analysis of what the text says explicitly as well as inferences drawn from the text.	W.7.2.A	Introduce a topic clearly, previewing what is to follow; organize ideas, concepts, and information, using strategies such as definition, classification, comparison/contrast, and cause/ effect; include formatting (e.g., headings), graphics (e.g., charts, tables), and multimedia when useful to aiding comprehension.
	R.I.7.4	Determine the meaning of words and phrases as they are used in a text, including figurative, connotative, and technical meanings; analyze the impact of a specific word choice on meaning and tone.	W.7.2.B	Develop the topic with relevant facts, definitions, concrete details, quotations, or other information and examples.
	R.I.7.6	Determine an author's point of view or purpose in a text and analyze	W.7.2.C	Use appropriate transitions to create cohesion and clarify the

MGRP Component	7th Grade English Language Arts Common Core State Standards: Reading		7th Grade English Language Arts Common Core State Standards: Writing	
		how the author distinguishes his or her position from that of others.		relationships among ideas and concepts.
	R.I.7.10	By the end of the year, read and comprehend literary nonfiction in the grades 6–8 text complexity band proficiently, with scaffolding as needed at the high end of the range.	W.7.2.D	Use precise language and domain-specific vocabulary to inform about or explain the topic.
			W.7.2.E	Establish and maintain a formal style.
			W.7.2.F	Provide a concluding statement or section that follows from and supports the information or explanation presented.
Poetry	RL.7.4	Determine the meaning of words and phrases as they are used in a text, including figurative and connotative meanings; analyze the impact of rhymes and other repetitions of sounds (e.g., alliteration) on a specific verse or stanza of a poem or section of a story or drama.	W.7.3.D	Use precise words and phrases, relevant descriptive details, and sensory language to capture the action and convey experiences and events.
	RL.7.5	Analyze how a drama's or poem's form or structure (e.g., soliloquy,		

MGRP Component	7th Grade English Language Arts Common Core State Standards: Reading		7th Grade English Language Arts Common Core State Standards: Writing	
		sonnet) contributes to its meaning.		
	RL.7.10	By the end of the year, read and comprehend literature, including stories, dramas, and poems, in the grades 6–8 text complexity band proficiently, with scaffolding as needed at the high end of the range.		
Combined MGRP	RL.7.7	Compare and contrast a written story, drama, or poem to its audio, filmed, staged, or multimedia version, analyzing the effects of techniques unique to each medium (e.g., lighting, sound, color, or camera focus and angles in a film).	W.7.4	Produce clear and coherent writing in which the development, organization, and style are appropriate to task, purpose, and audience.
	R.I.7.7	Compare and contrast a text to an audio, video, or multimedia version of the text, analyzing each medium's portrayal of the subject (e.g., how the delivery of a speech affects the impact of the words).	W.7.5	With some guidance and support from peers and adults, develop and strengthen writing as needed by planning, revising, editing, rewriting, or trying a new approach, focusing on how well purpose and audience have been addressed.
			W.7.7	Conduct short research projects to answer a question, drawing on

MGRP Component	7th Grade English Language Arts Common Core State Standards: Reading	7th Grade English Language Arts Common Core State Standards: Writing	
			several sources and generating additional related, focused questions for further research and investigation.
		W.7.8	Gather relevant information from multiple print and digital sources, using search terms effectively; assess the credibility and accuracy of each source; and quote or paraphrase the data and conclusions of others while avoiding plagiarism and following a standard format for citation.
		W.7.10	Write routinely over extended time frames (time for research, reflection, and revision) and shorter time frames (a single sitting or a day or two) for a range of discipline-specific tasks, purposes, and audiences.

References

Butler, J., & Bick, S. (2023). Audience awareness and access: The design of sound and captions as valuable composition practices. *College Composition and Communication, 74*(3), 416–445.

Cast. (2023, October 16). *The UDL guidelines.* https://udlguidelines.cast.org/

Choong, & Bjork, C. (2023). The student-podcaster as narrator of social change? *College Composition and Communication, 74*(3), 551–574.

Common core state standards initiative. (2023). https://corestandards.org/

Fisher, G. (2018). Evidence by the video method. *Journal of Legal Education, 68*(1), 15–22. https://www.jstor.org/stable/26890991

Kalantzis, M., & Cope, B. (2023). *Multiliteracies - New learning online.* New Learning Online. https://newlearningonline.com/multiliteracies/

National Council of Teachers of English. (2022, November 2). *Position statement on writing instruction in school.* https://ncte.org/statement/statement-on-writing-instruction-in-school/

Neville, M. (2023). "I want them to see writing as a joyful thing to do": Noticing texts as equity-oriented English education. *English Education, 55*(2), 92–115.

Nowell, Z. & Smith, A. (2023). Excavating erased histories as culturally sustaining instruction. *English Journal, 112*(4), 43–50.

Park, Y. J. (2023). Agency, identity, and writing: Perspectives from first-generation students of color in their first year of college. *Research in the Teaching of English, 57*(3), 227–247.

Rodríguez, E. (2023). Crossing into new sanctuaries: Poetic pedagogy for the often unseen. *English Journal, 112*(4), 28–34.

Romano, T. (1995). *Writing with passion: Life stories, multiple genres.* Boynton/Cook.

Romano, T. (2000). *Blending genre, altering style: Writing multigenre papers.* Boynton/Cook.

Romano, T. (2023). The truth about why I love to teach writing. *English Journal, 112*(4), 107–107.

Spinelli, H. (2023). Writing beyond borders: Latinx Voices in World Literature. *English Journal, 112*(4), 80–88.

Stringer, K. & Wiggers, A. (2023, May 25). *CHATGPT: Everything you need to know about the AI-powered chatbot.* TechCrunch. https://techcrunch.com/2023/05/24/chatgpt-everything-you-need-to-know-about-the-open-ai-powered-chatbot/

Turner, J. D., Wiseman, A. M., Coles, J., Jones, S. P., Cappello, M., Barton, R., Griffin, A. A., Rusoja, A., & Zapata, A. (2023). Mapping our truths--Envisioning the future of multimodal research for racial justice. *Research in the Teaching of English, 57*(3), 294–305.

Vázquez, A. (2023). Coming home: A reflection on the gift of poetry. *English Journal, 112*(4), 51–57.

Williamson, T. (2023). Experiences of alienation and intimacy: The work of secondary writing instruction. *Research in the Teaching of English, 57*(3), 271–293.

College Writing and
Teaching

Chapter 5

"So, I Thought This was a Writing Class!": Podcasting as Decolonized Knowledge Making

Jeaneen Canfield

University of Central Oklahoma

Abstract: Canfield discusses the use of podcasts and student reactions to the assignment. She also gives an answer to the question "Are podcasts academic writing?" Students have the opportunity to learn about audience and presentation as well as word-choice, making this an engaging way to teach students about what can count as academic writing.

Keywords: podcasts; academic writing; writing assignments

***

The student looked around at the class, suddenly realizing he was the only one raising his hand. "Boy! I've never been the 'smart' kid in the class before . . ." After completing a sound-composing assignment, I had just asked my students to indicate by way of raised hand which of them had felt comfortable with their finished projects. Only one student raised his hand. Struck by his obvious confidence, I, a multimodal scholar and writing instructor, was reminded of the reasons I continually ask students to compose multimodally.

I relate the above scenario because even now several years after my first encounter with multimodal compositional theories, I see the distinct opportunities that are available to us in writing pedagogy. My initial foray into multimodal composing began very early in my graduate career. I was introduced to and inspired by multimodal composing theories by the New London Group (1996). Additional scholars included Gunther Kress (2003, 2005), Patricia Dunn (2001), Cynthia Selfe (2009), Pamela Takayoshi and Cynthia Selfe (2007), Jason Palmeri

(2012), and Jody Shipka (2013), among others. Through multimodal scholarship, writing instruction has the potential to be at the forefront of curriculum changes that equip students for twenty-first-century communication practices. While conversations in Rhetoric and Writing Studies have discussed and (re)imagined what constitutes "writing" since before the 1990's, there are still current voiced concerns about the relevance of multimodal composing practices. For my purposes here, I draw from the above scholars and define multimodal composition as a composition comprised of 2 or more layers of communicative modes: words, still images, animation, video, and sound. While these compositions are many times contextualized in digital technologies, they (as Shipka reminds us) also move beyond the digital to include analog compositions as well.

In particular, multimodal compositions that take on audio formats are continuously called into question by both teachers and students alike. Jeremy Cushman and Shannon Kelly, in their 2018 chapter "Recasting Writing, Voicing Bodies: Podcasts across a Writing Curriculum," explain this long-tailed conversation. Quoting from Cynthia Selfe's 2009 foundational work, "The Movement of Air, the Breath of Meaning: Aurality and Multimodal Composing," Cushman and Kelly discuss the pervasive false binary between aurality and writing. Further, we are reminded of the concerns voiced by teachers who teach multimodal composing (Takayoshi & Selfe, 2007). In their chapter "Thinking about Multimodality," Takayoshi and Selfe explore concerns such as teachers wondering if they are really teaching composition at all if multimodal composing should be left to other disciplines, and if they need to become "technology expert[s], among other concerns" (9). Cushman and Kelly also explore the stories of their Graduate Teaching Assistants (GTA's) who teach first-year writing[1]. Many of those stories reflect concerns about the time invested, feelings of unsureness, assessment, and even concerns about what constitutes "academic" writing—all of which are legitimate concerns.

Composing in the 21st Century

My classroom experiences are very similar to those of many other scholars and teachers. Amidst the logistical concerns, though, I, too, have realized students' literacy growth in very interesting ways. Writing, in the twenty-first century, has become more broadly defined than its previous, more traditional definitions. It now includes meaning-making in nuanced ways, and writing assignments have taken on innovative forms such as webpages, podcasts, videos, and other digital forms, as well as material analog forms like mobiles, murals, etc. (Brandt, 2001, 2015; Selfe & Hawisher, 2004; Shipka, 2013). Further expanding

---

[1] Briefly, "first-year writing" courses at my institution are freshman-level, first and second semester writing courses as part of the General Education requirements.

writing teachers' understanding of language and meaning-making, translingual approaches delineate preconceived notions about language and identity. Such delineation potentially opens up possibilities for students to interrogate ways their languaging and identities are intertwined, as well as to explore innovative ways of knowledge-making (Cushman, 2016). In turn, such a disruption is now more possible than ever because multimodal writing assignments themselves potentially unsettle preconceived notions about what constitutes academic writing. If we accept such an exciting turn in writing studies pedagogy, what does that mean for assignment and activity designs? Furthermore, how might we continue to press forward toward a more democratic writing pedagogy?

To address these questions, I adopt a cultural rhetorics approach (Powell et al., 2014) and build on the rich foundation in writing studies. I merge that scholarship with indigenous pedagogical methodologies of listening and storytelling (King, 2005; King et al., 2015; Kovach, 2021) and explore an assignment designed for a first-year writing course that asks students to create a podcast. Indigenous scholar Lee Maracle (1994) argued that story and theory are so intertwined, that theory cannot be fully understood without story. I was born and raised in a minority-majority region (New Mexico and SW Colorado), so I have a deep appreciation for the power of stories. Through stories, we children shared familial experiences and traditions. Through these stories, I learned about world views different from my own, to be sure. But I also found connections between me and my Southern Ute, Diné, and Chicanx classmates. Through story, we grew to understand each other, to forge friendships, and to form our own community. While I am a cisgender, white female, my lived experience background calls me to recognize the value of indigenous methodologies. Indigenous methodologies call us to privilege intentional listening and stories as valid and important rhetorical moves, and it is through these practices that I am able to delineate power structures in my classroom so that students are empowered. In what follows, I identify my learning goals, describe the assignment, and explain the scaffolding activities. Finally, I theorize about the potential for decolonized writing pedagogy through assignments such as the one I discuss here.

Assignment Context

My first podcast assignment (distinct from an audio essay, which I will explain later) was in Spring 2016. Students were asked to explain their reading strategies when reading an academic article from their chosen field of study. One student selected an article about honey bees because she was majoring in Environmental Sciences. Similarly, the other students' projects centered around their interests and projected majors. I will not take the time and space here to elaborate on that particular assignment, but rather mention it as the starting point for the revised assignment that is the subject of this essay.

The assignment I now turn to is a podcast where students compose an analysis and proposal for a research source. To clarify what I mean here, there is a distinction between audio essays and podcasts. For me, an audio essay carries with it preconceived notions about formatting, structure, arrangement, and even word choice because of the word "essay." As Cushman and Kelly (2018) discuss, the term "essay" seems to immediately conjure up traditional ideas about writing, but the term "podcast" opens up new and interesting possibilities for embodied practices of writing that raise students' awareness of their personal writing voice and style. Drawing from rhetorical Genre Studies, the podcast genre connotes certain communicative features (Bawarshi and Reiff, 2010) that imply a particular approach to a composition project. Those characteristics mean the student writer considers the audience's needs, the intended purpose, and the most effective method for connecting the two. It also invokes an attitude of "play," which Brian Sutton-Smith (1997) asserts contributes to the productive possibilities of ambiguity. In other words, fostering an atmosphere of exploratory uncertainty can guide students toward substantial literacy growth. Additionally, James Paul Gee (2007) explains that for active learning to occur, students experience "the world in new ways" (p. 31), which is an essential component of effective, critical pedagogy. To put it succinctly, podcasts rely on speaker vocal inflections, musical transitions, and maybe even sound effects that all work together simultaneously. In fact, podcast scripts are increasingly used to broaden accessibility, and those scripts contain memos of each added communicative feature mentioned above. To that end, then, students compose a podcast instead of an audio essay.

This unit was the first step in scaffolding toward a larger researched argument that would be the final composition for the course. Prior to this assignment, I introduced students to the concept of multimodal composition: compositions created by layering two or more communicative modes (linguistic text, image text, audio text, movement, etc.). In my understanding of multimodal composing, I adopt *The New London Group's* (1996) explanation where "a multiplicity of discourses" (par. 2) or communicative modes operate simultaneously to communicate a message. I also drew from Jody Shipka's (2013) knowledge that multimodality does not necessarily mean digital compositions: it can be material analog as well. To provide context for the assignment, scaffolding lessons provided students the opportunity to examine photojournal essays, movie trailers, Soundscape essays, and 3-D Models. From their analysis of these compositions during class activities, they compiled a working list of techniques and strategies for composing multimodality.

At the beginning of the semester course, the initial concept I wanted my students to understand was the concept of "layers." I had students explore and identify their layered identities—the various identities outside of the classroom. These identities could include daughter, son, sister, nephew, athlete, musician, employee, and so on. We discussed how those layered lived experiences worked together to compose their overall identity. This concept of "layers" became the prior knowledge foundation I used to explain multimodal composition. Students then participated in threaded discussions and in-class activities where they examined multimodal forms such as memes, models, etc., and explored how meaning was communicated through the layered communicative modes working together. For one activity, they were to take a weekend and select one form of multimodal composition, take a picture, and upload the captured image into a discussion topic where I could show them during class discussion for us to analyze how the modes worked together. Students' images included billboards, posters, and user manuals, to name a few. I wanted students to gain an understanding of how they took in information before I had them compose in multimodality.

A final step of scaffolding I provided was to introduce students to archival research. I explored my institution's library to determine available archives, and I compiled a list of those archives. I also compile a list of digital archives. The list of digital archives includes archives that exemplify characteristics of reputable research sources. These archives are more than collections of artifacts (such as a baseball card archive). They are archives that contain various artifacts, contextual information, and collection methods. Attached as an Appendix here is a sampling of this list as the list is a living document that I continually evaluate and vet each semester to ensure all links work and the information is current.

After these activities, students were provided the podcast assignment as follows.

Assignment Steps

First, think about a broad research area for which you will write a researched argument later this semester (Composition #4). You do not have to know your specific research questions yet, just begin thinking about an area (subject) that interests you.

Second, select a digital or library research archive from the provided list to investigate (See Appendix). For this project, I am defining "archive" in this way: any "resource that collects and makes accessible materials for the purposes of research, knowledge building, or memory making" (Enoch and VanHaitsma, 2015, p. 4). The research sources I prefer for this assignment are **multimodal**: they include a selection of alphabetic, visual (still and moving), and/or oral texts. They can be digital or analog. You will thoroughly read and explore the archive, then write an analysis & proposal for it as a potential research source for your future research argument.

Third, you will compose a two-part composition that consists of an audio composition (podcast) wherein you analyze and propose the archive as one of your future sources for Composition #4 AND a formal Reflection.

PART A) Your Proposal Podcast is to be constructed in the following sections:

- INTRODUCTION – provide a general context for archives as research sources, your possible broad research topic, and your specific choice of archive
- ANALYSIS SECTION – guided by the following points of inquiry:
  - What is the subject and the stated purpose of the archive?
  - How does this archive fit into your proposed broad research topic?

Choose from ONE of the following to add to the above 2 points of inquiry:

  - The materials of the Archive offer a snapshot of a particular person, event, time, or place. Each of the items in the Archive offers a story or narrative. Which stories/which items are the most significant and why?

OR

  - Considering the voices present in the Archive, how are they a fair and equitable representation of the larger social/cultural context? In what ways might there be avenues for improvement?

- CONCLUSION SECTION – bring your proposal to a close by addressing the following points:

  - What are the ethical considerations/implications of the materials in this archive?
  - What are the shortcomings of this archive and how do you propose to continue your research and add other sources to this archive for your later researched argument?
  - Summarize and bring your Proposal to a close

PART B) Compose a 2-3-page reflection (story) where you consider the following 5 points:

- Why did you choose this archive and how did you approach/read it?
- What did you learn about the broad research area?
- What was your thinking and composing process when creating the Podcast Analysis/Proposal?
- What would you change if you did this assignment again?
- Reflect on the changes you made from your first draft to your final draft. Describe and explain those changes (points of literacy & writerly growth) for both the Podcast & the Reflection.

Fourth, upload your composition as well as the audio file or link to your Podcast into D2L.

And the learning goals for this assignment include the following:

- Identify and analyze the purpose, stance, and scope of a selected research source
- Develop and support an analytical proposal using evidence from the research source and course readings
- Demonstrate communicative skills for writing/communicating an effective proposal
- Identify and apply revision at both deep and surface levels, reflecting on literacy and writerly growth (your composing process story)

I handed out a printed copy of the full assignment sheet, as well as projected it from the LMS (Learning Management System) via the classroom projector. Together, we read through the requirements and expectations. Students' reactions were as multi-faceted as could be possibly imagined. There were questions about how this could be considered "serious writing" and something that they could use outside of this classroom. One student expressed that "this didn't really seem to provide anything helpful for her major, but that it was something she typically saw in an 'English class'" (her hands and fingers motioning the air quote marks). I allowed the students to gather in groups of 2 or 3 and voice their thoughts and questions about the assignment. I did this so I could observe student reactions and gauge levels of self-efficacy.

Reactions to the Assignment

Because I keep a teaching reflection journal, I record the results of my observations during class work. In my journal, I have recorded that I noticed in each of the three sections I was teaching that semester, there was a small number of students who expressed eager anticipation. They were the students who immediately turned to a neighbor and began discussing. I heard comments such as, "This is going to be cool!" and "I love listening to podcasts–I'm already thinking how I will create my own podcast!" I allowed the students to discuss for a few minutes, then I called them back to whole-class discussion and created a list on the board of their concerns. These concerns included the following:

- Little knowledge of technology
- How much time
- Length
- Not like sound of voice

They also, though, began talking about concerns typically associated with traditional writing assignments:

- How to structure
- How to arrange
- How to make sure "I'm clear"
- How long this should be

This second list is what really caught my attention because these are the things a writing teacher might typically teach. Instead, these students were coming up with questions about these things. I did not answer these questions directly but asked them back to the class in this way. First, I asked which students have listened to podcasts. In all of the classes I have taught, there have been around 2 or 3 students out of 20 who regularly listen to podcasts. In the past 3 years, this number has increased to 3 or 4 out of 20, which is still a significant minority of the constitutive whole. I then ask those students to provide us with the information they know about the structure, arrangement, and clarity of the podcasts from their experiences. We began making a list of "Tips and Strategies" which included the following:

- Music intro
- Welcome message
- Commercial breaks
- Musical transitions/interludes
- Sound effects
- Sections divided by point
- Conclusion
- Music closing

As any writing teacher knows, these insights are foundational to effective communication. The beauty of this was that the students, working together, constructed this list from their own experiential knowledge, and I did not have to devise a creative method for lecturing this information. In other words, the classroom had become a place of collaboratively constructed knowledge—a decentered learning environment.

Reflecting on the Classroom Data

It was at the closing of this class meeting introducing the podcast assignment that the question and response exchange I described in the epilogue occurred. Through the ensuing conversation, other students who had previously expressed their excitement about composing a podcast also found themselves as the "students-in-the-know." I distinctly recall two students who had introduced themselves to me at the beginning of the semester as students whose goal was to "get an 'A'" in the course (again referencing my reflective journal). These two students approached me after this class meeting and expressed their concern about potentially losing their "A" because of their unfamiliarity with podcast composing. I encouraged them to approach this assignment with the same work ethic they typically practiced and to also look forward to developing literacy growth. They left our conversation that day, expressing their doubt that this assignment would be useful to them beyond this class . . . I chose to allow them their resistance and see what the outcome might be.

Although this conversation exchange had the potential to color (dare I say "discolor") my eager anticipation for the literacy growth I hoped for my students, I decided to focus on the exciting possibilities I knew existed and press forward. I designed each class meeting to be a workshop, which means students worked in small groups to report their progress on their project since the last class meeting, identify the goals to complete before the next class meeting, and the challenges/problems they were experiencing. Calling the class to whole-class discussion, we collaboratively constructed a list of concerns (which I wrote on the board). I then asked for any student who could provide a solution for each challenge listed. Putting a student into this role of "expert" is, as good teachers understand, an empowering move that increases student efficacy. In this way, students, such as Kris (pseudonym for the student in the epilogue), who had never been identified as "smart" in their previous schooling experiences were now the experts in the room. This transferred to the next unit where these formally "hesitant" students were more confident as they approached their research topic and designed a research question.

Another empowering move I noticed was when the class discussed the "reflective story" which was the final step after the podcast. As a cultural rhetorician, I understand the significance of students' stories about their thinking and writing processes. Thomas King (2005) calls us to understand ways the story is a practice that is integral to developing identity and building knowledge. Joyce Rain Anderson (2015) explains the valuable contribution indigenous epistemologies can have on the writing classroom. The stories we tell reveal the compilations of our layered identity and listening to others' stories changes us, the listener. The practice of listening is invaluable for me as a teacher when I privilege students' voices above my own. The emerging phenomena in my classroom indicated that students who had typically been characterized as "hesitant" or "quiet" learners/students became confident and engaged learners/students. Story and listening became integral to my pedagogical approach.

For my students who come from backgrounds where story is an essential practice, this listening move is expected. For my students who do not come with this background knowledge, there is a tendency for them to classify a reflective story as non-academic writing. During the class meeting where we discussed Part B of the assignment, a few students (who had in one way or another told me they had never earned anything lower than an "A") voiced concerns about not only the podcast being non-serious writing, but now the reflective story was also less-than-serious academic writing. I decided to take the opportunity to explain the value of a story as knowledge-sharing. In my mini-lecture, I briefly explained two acts of storytelling: 1) telling the story, and 2) listening to the story. I also explained how indigenous cultures have practiced cultural sustainability through storytelling, as well as strengthened communal connections. Several of my students had not ever seriously considered a story as a complex composition, which allowed for further conversations and discussions about ways stories might be used as frameworks for future academic writings outside of our classroom.

Conclusion

I noted in my reflective journal that several students who had background knowledge about story interjected their experiences with the story as a mode for conveying information and building connections between an audience and speaker. Therefore, as one student so eloquently stated, this could be perhaps the most important part of this entire composition because it allowed her to explain the specific techniques and strategies she used in her podcast, which made her feel "important and knowledgeable as an academic writer" (reflective journal). This, to my mind, is exactly what Maracle (1994) espouses when she asserts the value of story as a theory to explain phenomena.

Another fruitful outcome of this podcast assignment was the students' reaction to "play." I introduced anchor.fm (now "podcasters.spotify.com") as a platform for the students to create their podcasts. This site has everything a novice podcaster needs to create and publish a podcast or save the audio file (for students who were hesitant to make their compositions public). I set aside class time for students to explore the musical transitions and backgrounds. They worked in class with a partner and created a 30-second podcast introducing each other. This introduction had to be set to background music. I noticed that most students became excited about the upcoming assignment when they realized the ease with which they could use this platform to create their composition. We also took the time to listen to each other's mini-podcasts. Students asked questions of those groups whose podcasts evidenced more sophisticated uses of the musical transitions or vocal nuances. There was laughter and an overall sense of anticipation by the end of this class meeting. This time of play and experimentation allowed students a low-stakes opportunity to experiment with a composing process about which they had little to no knowledge. In my mind, this was exactly what Sutton-Smith (1997) and Gee (2007) are calling teachers to embrace, namely the productive potential of "play."

As several of my students clearly demonstrate, the podcast and reflective story assignment turned my writing classroom upside down in many ways. The assignment disrupts expected notions about "academic writing" because it is an audio and a story—both of which can be doubted to be used beyond an English classroom. Keep in mind that this assignment was a formal proposal with analysis, and the reflective story was an introspective rationale. Both of these are built on underpinning skills that are essential for academic growth and knowledge-building. For the students who were never able to make the move to embrace the podcast and the reflective story as academic writing, their compositions were less thoughtful and sophisticated. As I move forward with this assignment and others like it, I am committed to exploring ways to disrupt students' preconceived notions about academic writing so that they can potentially experience a never-ending literacy growth.

Overall, the podcast assignment provided students the opportunity to think about writing in more nuanced ways. It also, while disrupting their preconceived notions about a writing class, stimulated creativity and fostered critical thinking in very productive ways. The stories these students told, through their podcasts and their reflections, offered me (their writing instructor) valuable insight into their composing/thinking practices, thus providing me data to evaluate and strengthen my pedagogical approaches.

Appendix

Sample List of Digital Archives

Please note: For the purposes of this class (ENGL 1213), we define digital archive as: "…any digital resource that collects and makes accessible materials for the purposes of research, knowledge building, or memory making" (Enoch and Van Haitsma 4). In addition, the digital archives we prefer for this assignment are **multi**modal: they include a selection of traditional alphabetic, visual (still and moving), and/or oral texts. They are "dynamic sites of rhetorical power" (Morris qtd. in Enoch and Van Haitsma 3) and therefore collections featuring more than one mode will be more effective than a single mode. For example, an archive of baseball cards and only baseball cards will not have enough variety of information/artifacts to provide useful material for this course's learning outcomes.

Events

AIDS History Project

The UCSF Archives and Special Collections department has played a key role in documenting the AIDS epidemic. In 1987, the Archives & Special Collections initiated, in collaboration with the Gay, Lesbian, Bisexual, Transgender Historical Society (GLBHT HS) and the University of California, Berkeley, the AIDS History Project. The purpose of this initiative was to actively collect and organize papers and records of healthcare practitioners, activists, organizations, and agencies, and to promote the preservation of historically significant resources related to the beginning of the AIDS epidemic in San Francisco. https://www.library.ucsf.edu/archives/aids/

Densho Archive

"Densho's mission is to preserve the testimonies of Japanese Americans who were unjustly incarcerated during World War II before their memories are extinguished. We offer these irreplaceable firsthand accounts, coupled with historical images and teacher resources, to explore principles of democracy, and promote equal justice for all." https://densho.org/about-densho/

The Gun Violence Archive

"Gun Violence Archive (GVA) is a not-for-profit corporation formed in 2013 to provide free online public access to accurate information about gun-related violence in the United States. GVA will collect and check for accuracy, comprehensive information about gun-related violence in the U.S. and then post and disseminate it online." https://www.gunviolencearchive.org/

Hurricane Digital Memory Bank

"Launched in 2005, the *Hurricane Digital Memory Bank* uses electronic media to collect, preserve, and present the stories and digital record of Hurricanes Katrina and Rita." https://hurricanearchive.org/

Influenza Encyclopedia: The American Influenza Epidemic of 1918-19

An estimated 650,000 Americans lost their lives to the infamous and tragic 1918-1919 influenza epidemic, a small but significant fraction of the approximately 50 million deaths the disease caused worldwide. Countless more were left without parents, children, friends, and loved ones. Communities across the country did what they could to stem the rising tide of illness and death, closing their schools, churches, theaters, shops, and saloons. Doctors, nurses, and volunteers gave their time – and, occasionally, their lives – to care for the ill. These pages contain the stories of the places, the people, and the organizations that battled the American influenza epidemic of 1918-1919." https://www.influenzaarchive.org/

Alternative Considerations of Jonestown and People's Temple

"This website is designed to give personal and scholarly perspectives on a major event in the history of religion in America. Its primary purpose is to present information about Peoples Temple as accurately and objectively as possible. In an effort to be impartial, we offer many diverse views and opinions about the Temple and the events in Jonestown." https://jonestown.sdsu.edu/

Kent State Shootings Digital Archive

Contains photographs, scans of letters, audio recordings, and other documents related to the May 4, 1970 shooting of four Kent State University students during the Viet Nam War protests. https://omeka.library.kent.edu/special-collections/kent-state-shootings-digital-archive

Nuremberg Trials Project

"Examine trial transcripts, briefs, document books, evidence files, and other papers from the trials of military and political leaders of Nazi Germany." https://nbg-02.lil.tools/

Our Marathon: The Boston Bombing Digital Archive

"Our Marathon is a crowd-sourced, digital archive of pictures, videos, stories, and social media related to the Boston Marathon bombing." http://marathon.library.northeastern.edu/

Salmon in the Pacific Northwest and Alaska Collection 1890-1961

Salmon in the Northwest contains documents, photographs and other original material describing the roots of the salmon crisis in the Pacific Northwest in the late 19th and early 20th centuries. https://content.lib.washington.edu/salmonweb/index.html

The September 11 Digital Archive

"The September 11 Digital Archive uses electronic media to collect, preserve, and present the history of September 11, 2001 and its aftermath." http://911digitalarchive.org/

The Stanford Prison Experiment Collection

"Carried out August 15-21, 1971 in the basement of Jordan Hall, the Stanford Prison Experiment set out to examine the psychological effects of authority and powerlessness in a prison environment. The study, led by psychology professor Philip G. Zimbardo, recruited Stanford students using a local newspaper ad.

Twenty-four students were carefully screened and randomly assigned into groups of prisoners and guards. The experiment, which was scheduled to last 1-2 weeks, ultimately had to be terminated on only the 6th day as the experiment escalated out of hand when the prisoners were forced to endure cruel and dehumanizing abuse at the hands of their peers. The experiment showed, in Dr. Zimbardo's words, how "ordinary college students could do terrible things." This collection includes video, audio, photographs, and articles about the experiment and its aftermath. https://exhibits.stanford.edu/spe/browse

Tacoma Narrows Bridge Collection

Known mainly for its infamous collapse in 1940, the Tacoma Narrows Bridge continues to hold a place in engineering and Pacific Northwest history. This collection contains images and text drawn from the University of Washington Special Collections Division and the Museum of History and Industry. They document the creation of the Tacoma Narrows Bridge, its collapse and subsequent studies involving its aerodynamics, and finally the construction of a second bridge spanning the Narrows. https://content.lib.washington.edu/farquharso nweb/index.html

Tulsa Race Riot Archive

"This collection details one of the darkest episodes in Oklahoma History. The 1921 Tulsa Race Riot constituted two days of violence that left an unconfirmed number of dead citizens and destroyed 35 square blocks of the prosperous Greenwood neighborhood, once known as "Black Wall Street." It never recovered." http://digitalprairie.ok.gov/cdm/landingpage/collection/race-riot

1921 Tulsa Race Massacre Centennial Commission

From the "Who We Are" link on this site: "The 1921 Tulsa Race Massacre Centennial Centennial will leverage the rich history surrounding the 1921 Tulsa Race Massacre by facilitating actions, activities, and events that commemorate and educate all citizens." Several projects are included in this educational archive illuminating the Massacre's impact on the state of Oklahoma. https://www.tul sa2021.org/

Cinders in the Sky

The Legacy of the Tulsa Race Massacre. This archive was created by graduate students in a Digital Humanities class at Oklahoma State University. Here, there are collections of stories, interviews, and much more that provide a thorough investigation into this horrific event. https://oms.library.okstate.edu/s/introdu ction-to-digital-humanities/page/home

The Yad Vashem World Holocaust Remembrance Center

"Since its establishment, the Archive has initiated activities with a view to collecting and copying Holocaust related documents that have been housed in

various archives in Europe and throughout the world." http://www.yadvashem
.org/

People

Aldo Leopold Archive

"Aldo Leopold is considered by many to have been the most influential
conservation thinker of the 20th Century. Leopold's legacy spans the disciplines
of forestry, wildlife management, conservation biology, sustainable agriculture,
restoration ecology, private land management, environmental history, literature,
education, esthetics, and ethics. He is most widely known as the author of *A
Sand County Almanac*, one of the most beloved and respected books about the
environment ever published. The Leopold Collection houses the raw materials
that document not only Leopold's rise to prominence but the history of
conservation and the emergence of the field of ecology from the early 1900s
until his death in 1948." https://uwdc.library.wisc.edu/collections/aldoleopold/

The Michael Collins Papers

"The collection includes the papers of Michael Collins--pilot, astronaut, assistant
secretary of state, director of the National Air and Space Museum and author,
dating from 1907-2004. Materials include reports, instruction manuals, personal
notes, printed materials, audio recordings, photographs, awards and memorabilia
associated with Collins' Air Force, NASA, State Department and NASM careers.
There are also papers and research relating to Collins' writings; materials from
public speaking engagements and board and club memberships; and small sets
of personal correspondence and biographical material." https://digitalsc.lib.vt.
edu/Ms1989-029

The Dreyfus Affair

The Dreyfus Affair describes the accusation of treason and the subsequent trial
of Captain Dreyfus. Marked by anti-semitism, prejudice, forgery, and lies, the
Affair was a major world event "All of the major events of the Affair, from the
wrongful conviction of Captain Alfred Dreyfus for treason in 1894, to Emile
Zola's galvanizing statement headlined 'J'Accuse . . .!' in 1898, to Dreyfus' long
awaited exoneration in 1906 are represented by original items in the collection.
The power of print media was crucial in swaying public opinion during the
Affair, and the Collection contains many examples of the diverse genres and
formats of printed matter from the period. These include posters, broadsides,
newspapers, magazines, prints, caricatures, books, and postcards. In addition
to highlighting the crucial role of the media in the Affair, these documents
remain provocative and visually arresting even over a century later. The Collection
also includes original correspondence, photographs, and material artifacts
which record the impact of the Affair in its own time and help document its

memorialization through the subsequent decades." http://sceti.library.upenn. edu/dreyfus/index.cfm

The Earhart Project

This archive is a collection of materials related to the mysterious disappearance of Amelia Earhart, the famous American pilot. https://tighar.org/Projects/Earh art/AEdescr.html

Mark Twain Project Online

"Mark Twain Project Online applies innovative technology to more than four decades' worth of archival research by expert editors at the Mark Twain Project. It offers unfettered, intuitive access to reliable texts, accurate and exhaustive notes, and the most recently discovered letters and documents.

Its ultimate purpose is to produce a digital critical edition, fully annotated, of everything Mark Twain wrote." https://www.marktwainproject.org/

Minnie Fisher Cunningham Papers

"This extensive digital collection documents the activities of Minnie Fisher Cunningham and other leading suffragists who pushed for equal voting rights for women, culminating in the passage and ratification of the 19th Amendment to the United States Constitution. Dated mostly from 1917-1919, the materials include correspondence, pamphlets, flyers, speeches, newspaper articles, photographs, and legislative measures. Many of the 518 items in the collection contain multiple pages." https://findingaids.lib.uh.edu/repositories/2/resourc es/232

Oliver Wendall Holmes, Jr. (Supreme Court Justice) Digital Suite

"The Oliver Wendell Holmes, Jr. Digital Suite offers unprecedented access to the Harvard Law School Library's rich collection of Holmes archival material." http://library.law.harvard.edu/suites/owh/

Nikola Tesla Museum

This archive is a collection of Tesla's personal documents, manuscripts, scientific notes, calculations, diagrams, and more. https://tesla-museum.org/en/legacy /archive/.
The main page for the online museum is found here: https://nikolateslamuseu m.org/en/

Nikola Tesla's Archive

Nikola Tesla's Archive consists of a unique collection of manuscripts, photographs, and scientific and patent documentation which is indispensable in studying the history of electrification of the whole Globe. https://en.unesco.org/memor yoftheworld/registry/506

The Turing Digital Archive

"Alan Turing (1912-54) is best-known for helping decipher the code created by German Enigma machines in the Second World War, and for being one of the founders of computer science and artificial intelligence. This archive contains many of Turing's letters, talks, photographs, and unpublished papers, as well as memoirs and obituaries written about him. It contains images of the original documents that are held in the Turing collection at King's College, Cambridge." http://www.alanturing.net/

Places

Chilocco History Project

"The Chilocco Indian Agricultural School, located in north central Oklahoma, operated from 1884 -1980 as one of a handful of federal off-reservation Indian boarding schools in the United States. Thousands of students passed through the school's iconic entryway arch during its nearly century-long existence. Even today, Chilocco continues to be a powerful site for memory for its remaining alumni from over 127 tribes, as well as the Native peoples, directly or indirectly impacted by its history and scholars and students throughout the world who seek to understand its role within the larger context of U.S. Indian boarding schools. The work seen here represents a two year collaborative project between the Chilocco National Alumni Association (CNAA) and the Oklahoma Oral History Research Program (OOHRP) at the Oklahoma State University Library." https://chilocco.library.okstate.edu/

Greenwich Village History

"GVSHP offers a variety of tools to help you learn more about the history and culture of our neighborhoods, help in the fight to preserve Greenwich Village, the East Village, and NoHo, and find out more about preservation in New York City and beyond." https://www.villagepreservation.org/_gvshp/resources/index.htm

New Mexico History Digital Archive

"New Mexico Digital Collections is the central search portal for digital collections about New Mexico. A service of the University of New Mexico Libraries, we provide access to digitized photographs, manuscripts, posters, oral histories, videos, maps, and books from libraries, museums, and cultural centers across the state." http://econtent.unm.edu/

Bracero History Archive

"The *Bracero History Archive* collects and makes available the oral histories and artifacts pertaining to the Bracero program, a guest worker initiative that spanned the years 1942-1964. Millions of Mexican agricultural workers crossed

the border under the program to work in more than half of the states in America."
http://braceroarchive.org/

Utah American Indian Digital Archive

"The Utah American Indian Digital Archive (UAIDA) is a gateway to the best resources regarding Utah's Indian tribes. With articles, books, government documents, tribal documents, oral histories, photographs, and maps pertaining to the Northwestern Shoshone, Goshute, Paiute, Utah Navajo, White Mesa, and Ute Indians, this unique archive captures the complicated history of Utah's tribes from multiple perspectives." https://utahindians.org/archives/

The Digital Archive of Caribbean and Latin American Ephemera

"...a steadily growing repository containing a previously unavailable subset of Princeton's Latin American Ephemera Collection as well as newly acquired materials being digitized and added on an ongoing basis. The bulk of the materials currently found in the Digital Archive were originally created around the turn of the 20th century and after, with some originating as recently as within the last year." You will need to read Spanish in order to research this archive. http://library.princeton.edu/resource/14503

References

Anderson, J. R. (2015). Remapping settler colonial territories: Bringing local native knowledge into the classroom. *Survivance, sovereignty, and story,* (pp. 160-169). U of CO Press.

Bawarshi, A. S. and M. J. Reiff. (2010). *Genre: An introduction to history, theory, research, and pedagogy.* Parlor Press.

Brandt, D. (2001). *Literacy in American lives.* Cambridge.

Brandt, D. (2015). *The rise of writing: Redefining mass literacy.* Cambridge.

Cushman, E. (2016). Translingual and decolonial approaches to meaning making. *College English, 78*(3), 234-242. https://www.proquest.com/docview/1750722334/abstract/B490A8F71880492DPQ/1

Cushman, J., & Kelly, S. (2018). Recasting writing, voicing bodies: Podcasts across a writing curriculum. In C. S. Danforth, K. Stedman, & M. J. Faris (Eds.) *Soundwriting pedagogies.* Computers and Composition Digital Press. https://ccdigitalpress.org/book/soundwriting/cushman-kelly/index.html

Dunn, P. (2001). *Talking, sketching, moving: multiple literacies in the teaching of writing.* Boynton/Cook.

Enoch, J. & VanHaitsma, P. (2015). Archival literacy: Reading the rhetoric of digital archives in the undergraduate classroom. *College Composition and Communication, 67*(2), 216-242. https://library.ncte.org/journals/CCC/issues/v67-2/27643

Gee, J. P. (2007). *What video games have to teach us about learning and literacy.* Palgrave Macmillan.

King, L., Gubele, R., & Anderson, J. R. (Eds). (2015). Careful with the stories we tell: Naming survivance, sovereignty, and story. In *Survivance, sovereignty, and story* (pp. 3-16). U of CO Press.

King, T. (2005). *The truth about stories.* U of MN Press.

Kovach, M. (2021). *Indigenous methodologies: Characteristics, conversations, and contexts.* U of Toronto Press.

Kress, G. (2003). *Literacy in the new media age.* Routledge.

Kress, G. (2005). Gains and losses: New forms of texts, knowledge, and learning. *Computers and Composition, 22*(1), 5-22. https://doi.10.1016/j.compcom.2004.12.004

Maracle, L. (1994). Oratory: Coming to theory. *Essays on Canadian Writing,* (54), 7-11. https://libproxy.uco.edu/login?url=https://www.proquest.com/scholarly-journals/oratory-coming-theory/docview/197245877/se-2

New London Group. (1996). A pedagogy of multiliteracies: Designing social futures. *Harvard Educational Review, 66*(1). https://www.sfu.ca/~decaste/newlondon.htm

Palmeri, J. (2012). *Remixing composition: A history of multimodal writing pedagogy.* Southern IL U Press.

Powell, M., Levy, D., Riley-Mukavetz, A., Brooks-Gillies, M., Novotny, M., & Fisch-Ferguson, J. (2014). Our story begins here: Constellating cultural rhetorics. *Enculturation: A journal of rhetoric, writing, and culture.* http://enculturation.net/our-story-begins-here

Selfe, C. (2009). The movement of air, the breath of meaning: Aurality and multimodal composing. *College Composition and Communication, 60*(4), 616-663. http://www.jstor.org/stable/40593423

Selfe, C. L. & Hawisher, G. E. (2004). *Literate lives in the information age.* Routledge.

Shipka, J. (2013). Including, but not limited to, the digital: Composing multimodal texts. In T. Bowen & C. Whithaus (Eds.) *Multimodal literacies and emerging genres,* (pp. 73-89). Pittsburgh Press.

Sutton-Smith, B. (1997). *The ambiguity of play.* Harvard UP.

Takayoshi, P. & Selfe, C. (2007). Thinking about multimodality. In C. Selfe (Ed.), *Multimodal Composition: Resources for Teachers* (pp. 1-12). Hampton Press.

Chapter 6

Teaching Composition through Digital Game Design

Lia Schuermann
Texas Woman's University

Abstract: Schuermann focuses on games and how they can be used in the higher education classroom. Games have the potential for rich literacy and learning practices (Gee; Custer; Juul), and game designers, like course designers, create experiences with problem-solving, creativity, and interpretive play (Robison; Ballentine; Custer). Building from the work of frontier teacher-scholars, this chapter presents a themed first-year composition course based on digital game design and development that utilizes digital games' affordances. This chapter further describes the course's activities, examples, and resources to support four major writing assignments based in digital game composition writing and collaborative writing. Then the chapter concludes with the feedback, implications, and suggestions for instructors interested in engaging students in creative ways and in developing their own writing courses based on digital game design and development.

Keywords: games; higher education; first-year composition; collaborative writing

***

Introduction

Why teach students about digital game design in the composition classroom? Students are used to composing traditional academic essays, but games provide an alternative medium that students can engage in with curiosity, creativity, and play. It creates new experiences for students and enables them to compose with the multimodal aspects of game design. They also take on the role of a game designer, and just like those in the game industry, they write collaboratively with their peers to problem-solve, create, and play.

While 'video games' is a more familiar term, 'digital games' functions to more accurately represent games made for platforms beyond consoles, such as computers (PC, Mac, Linux, etc.) and mobile operating systems (Android & iOS). While digital games are published by both large and small companies, they are generally made by a team of game designers who have distinct roles in the team. This can range from story-writing to concept art design to music composers. They also tend to have a project lead or manager, a role that the instructor takes on to help facilitate the teams that are formed within the course.

Furthermore, digital games have a variety of multimodal elements. Some of these are more familiar to composition instructors, such as sound/music, visuals/graphic design, and text/font. But others may be new concepts involving gameplay and game mechanics. Gameplay is what occurs in the game, the actual interaction between the player and the game. Game mechanics are the game rules that conceptualize how the player can interact within the game (objectives, actions, perspective, etc.) that tend to define what genre the game belongs to. These can be hard to distinguish from each other since they intrinsically intersect, but it is important to tell them apart and designate their appropriate elements when designing a game to be understood by team members and player audiences.

And just like traditional writing from rhetorical analysis to an argument paper, game compositions have genres with different audiences and purposes. Whether to gain sponsorship or funding, game development teams usually develop a game pitch for their designs. These tend to be multimodal presentations, even when the game design is not necessarily fully fleshed out and illustrate the general design and core concepts of the game, along with the core mechanics, themes, story, and gameplay. Once teams begin to build their game design further, this becomes the document that is used within the team to communicate and collaborate in developing their game and to present and update the publisher/sponsor.

Literature Review

Gamification, defined as applying the unique, accessible, competitive, and cooperative elements of games to course design (Slentz, et al., 2017, pp. 185), has become a new pedagogical trend, especially within the field of composition. With gamification, teachers recognize games' unique affordances of interactivity and rules-based and achievement-focused structure that can be utilized in creating a curriculum within that structure or applying parts of it. However, a large part of this affordance is the design of the games themselves. Concerns about gamification have risen for instructors outside of game studies, particularly in the field of rhetoric and composition, utilizing shallow aspects of games such as badges, points, and leaderboards rather than its more powerful affordances of engagement, interactivity, and storytelling (McGunnigle, 2023, pp. xxxv-xxxvi).

As Alice J. Robison (2008) states, "It is the nascent field of game studies that has brought to bear the very quality that makes games unique: their ability to inspire a host of interactive meaning-making experiences designed with the purpose of engaging players in immersive, cognitively and socially complex worlds and situations" (p. 359). While the field of game studies is still relatively new, their concepts of interactivity and ludo narrativity clarify the way games are designed to engage players through immersive experiences and support core themes and mechanics. This parallels the ways in which writers seek to engage their audiences and how each element of a composition seeks to support a main idea and purpose. Additionally, Jesper Juul's (2003) definition of games, built from research on the history of games and their previous definitions, helps to define the medium's features to enable composition instructors and their students to understand digital games discretely from other mediums and to better analyze and build work with games' defined features.

These unique features and affordances have led digital games to be utilized in course designs (Ballentine, 2015; Custer, 2013; Robison, 2008) and show that games have the potential for rich literacy and learning practices (Custer, 2013; Gee, 2003; Juul, 2003). Additionally, Gee (2003), Custer (2013), and Colby (2017) demonstrate the ways games' multimodality extends beyond the usual scope with its interactivity and game mechanics which functions to build students' multimodal literacy in the classroom, especially for composition courses based on game design.

Game designers, much like course designers, create experiences where problem-solving, creativity, and interpretive play take place (Ballentine, 2015; Custer, 2013; Robison, 2008). Ballentine (2015) explains in these kinds of courses that "It will be the writing instructor's job as teacher and manager to lead students through the creative and subjective messiness of development" (p. 35). The instructor works to facilitate the team's creative process to be equitable, help them problem-solve through challenges, and orient their play at designing a game.

This communication between instructor and student, as well as students with each other, also points out the nature of digital game writing to be a collaborative space. Jonathan Alexander (2009), a composition scholar and teacher who utilizes games in his own teaching, discusses how writing, particularly in professional spaces, is collaborative, written within a conversation of others' perspectives and ideas. Games work to emphasize the collaborative nature of writing that is a natural part of the game design composing process and to showcase the ways writing, even when written by a single individual, is not composed in isolation.

Part of this collaborative writing is building a community within the classroom. Chris McGunnigle (2023), a rhetoric and composition scholar who has written on gamification in course curriculum, states that the "introduction of a new discourse [guides] students into a coherent and unified conversation around their uncertainties and need for knowledge" (pp. xxxi). Digital games work as a new discourse that students in the classroom can build community around by relying not only on the instructor but each other to address gaps and concerns about an unfamiliar discourse. Even students who are familiar with playing games will more than likely still lack knowledge of game design aspects and thus will be engaging with a new discourse along with their peers. This also works to address inequities associated with background knowledge and past experience with academic discourse and spaces, as students engage this new discourse from a similar starting point and must work together to support one another in navigating it.

Scaffolding

To begin with, I designed a themed first-year composition (FYC) course that I taught for Fall 2022 and Spring 2023 for approximately 23 students per course. Our FYC program consists of two consecutive courses with the latter focusing more on argumentation and research, which I taught with this themed framework. As Ballentine (2015) asserts, "[F]or an undergraduate course that assume[s] no prior experience with games or their development, a comfortable place to begin [i]s much needed" (p. 33). And so, scaffolding of game design concepts is necessary alongside scaffolding for writing concepts in the classroom.

To ensure an understanding of game design concepts, I began my course with a focus on genres of writing and other media before focusing on digital game genres through collaborative discussions and resources. As part of this scaffolding, my class plays and analyzes games throughout the semester. This scaffolding consists of an in-class activity and a homework assignment.

In the in-class activity, I provide digital games, such as *Baba is You, Lutong Bahay: Lola's Home Cooking*, and *Chicory: A Colorful Tale*, from my personal library on Steam or Itch.io to showcase certain game aspects that range from genres to unique game & game play mechanics to various kinds of storytelling. From there, I ask a student to volunteer to play the game and provide a community Google Doc for the rest of the class to participate in while they observe the gameplay. This Google Doc consists of questions about various game aspects and rhetorical aspects that students can answer through observation, evaluation, and analysis. Questions are assigned to small groups. I give them some time to observe and analyze, and then my students discuss what they observed and their analysis, including follow-up questions to determine students' personal thoughts and observations to aid their understanding and application of digital game aspects in their major assignments.

For homework, I provide a curated list of no-cost games for students to choose from (which range from game demos to full game releases). This list is organized based on game aspects and genres that these games showcase and are scaffolded with the digital game design resources and focus for each week in the course. This curated list provides accessible choices for students to choose from based on their available platforms, including PC, Mac, Linux, Android, and iOS. There are also games that can be played from web browsers without any downloads, which students can play from the university's library computers if necessary. Then, students must answer reflection questions about game design and rhetorical aspects of the game they chose to play (refer to Figure 6.1 for examples of these questions).

Figure 6.1. Example Analysis/Reflection Questions

- What game did you play?
- What genre was the game? How did this game's moves follow or not follow the moves of its genre?
- What did you think of the games? What did you like or dislike? Be specific.
- What were the games' goals and objectives? How do you reach these goals?
- What are you expected to do as the player (mechanics)?
- How did it feel to play the game? Were you satisfied with the gameplay?
- What would you do differently if you were able to make changes to the game design?
- What message do you think the game/s are trying to communicate to the player through each of these aspects?
- How did the game's mechanics and/or genre reinforce or weaken this message?
- Who do you think is the intended audience for this game? For what purpose do you think this game was made?
- What aspects of these games might you consider writing about for your game think piece or explore in future writing?

To help further address gaps in knowledge about game design and development, I also provide accessible resources that I have curated to support students. This includes game development team devlogs & interviews, design talks by developers and designers, examples of design documents, and interdisciplinary scholars discussing game design and its potential in research and pedagogical spaces. These resources range in form from YouTube videos to scholarly articles to game magazine articles. These are generally assigned for homework and discussed in class, where I give them time to review the assigned readings/resources, discuss them in small groups by table, and then discuss them as a class.

Major Assignments

My first major assignment is an individually-assigned game think piece, which is a public-facing genre of writing that focuses on being thought-provoking and on personal opinion, background, and analysis. I chose this assignment for several reasons. I considered that students were probably just beginning to become familiar with game design aspects, and I wanted to choose a writing genre that didn't rely too heavily on game design knowledge. Also, I thought a think piece would work well with the subsequent major assignments since they all work more towards a public-facing audience outside of academia and function within alternative yet professional writing spaces.

The purpose of this game think piece is to serve as a first big step for students to engage with game design and development while also considering audience, purpose, and genre in their composition. The 'game' part of this assignment involves engaging in conversations and issues within gaming communities about an aspect of digital games. The aforementioned scaffolding aids students to become more familiar with digital game aspects and with game think piece examples to learn how to create their own game think pieces. Part of this scaffolding begins in week one with a multimodal activity in Google Slides where they state their favorite game and explain what aspects of the game made it their favorite. The writing assignment asks students to consider what personal stake they have in their chosen topic of conversation, different perspectives and sources, and specific suggestions for their chosen audience along with the purpose and rhetorical situation of their game think piece.

And so, this activity helps students to consider what matters to them when it comes to game design and how they have a stake in conversations that involve those aspects of their favorite game. An interesting note here is that I have never had a student state that they've never played a digital game before. Sometimes students do not realize they have played a digital game since connotations of 'video games' tend to have people think of more modern games and game genres, but I believe (while based on local experience) this showcases the ways in which digital games have become so prevalent in our daily lives.

Furthermore, the weeks spent building their game design knowledge so that they could write the game think piece culminated in filling in their knowledge gaps to prepare them for their second major assignment, the individually-assigned game pitch. At first teaching, the game pitch was more difficult than I anticipated since the game pitch I was asking for from students used more direct references to experts and sources than professional examples of game pitches utilized. These professional examples also differed in manners of organization and in what content was more focused on.

What ended up being essential to clarifying assignment expectations and supporting their understanding of the game pitch genre was developing a game pitch myself, as a closer example of the game pitch I was asking for (refer to Appendix A for this example game pitch). I present the pitch in class and break down each of my rhetorical choices, including font, color choice/palette, organization pattern, sources, game mechanics, and visuals. I explain to my students that they are making rhetorical choices in the game and the pitch they are designing. Another element of the game pitch that is significant in explaining the genre to them is that a game pitch's purpose is to give the core concept (or main idea) of the game they are pitching and that they need not detail every aspect of the game. This also is important because if their pitch is chosen as part of the third major assignment, the game proposal, it would leave room for team members to contribute to the game design.

An important note here is that beginning with the game pitch, the major assignments begin to separate into two tracks, A and B (refer to Figure 6.2 for a visual for these assignment tracks). While the game pitch is nearly identical whether students chose track A or B, the audiences are different as they lead to drastically different major assignments for the third and fourth major assignments. Track A focuses more on teamwork and collaborative writing with their peers as one of their target audiences for the game pitch. On the other hand, track B aligns more closely with traditional academic writing genres but still focuses on game design aspects and multimodality, with a specific game developer studio as the target audience, pitching their game design for them to potentially develop.

Figure 6.2. Visual for Assignment Tracks

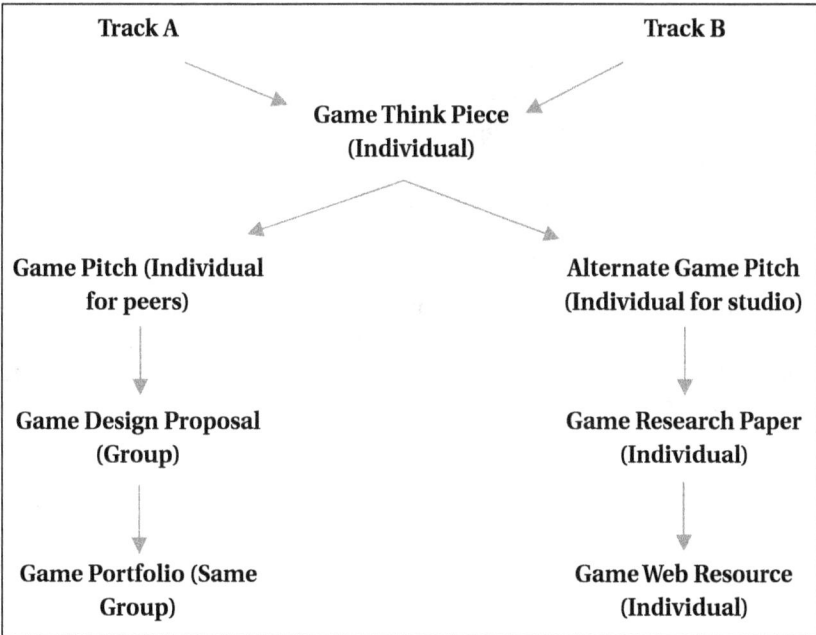

Track A		**Track B**
	Game Think Piece (Individual)	
Game Pitch (Individual for peers)		**Alternate Game Pitch (Individual for studio)**
Game Design Proposal (Group)		**Game Research Paper (Individual)**
Game Portfolio (Same Group)		**Game Web Resource (Individual)**

Structuring the course design like this is important in allowing students agency in what kinds of writing they choose to focus on, especially because our themed composition courses do not differ from traditional composition courses when students register for them. I do email students about the theme before the course starts but with late registration, drops, and students not always reading instructors' emails, they are not always aware before the first day of class of the theme. Additionally, students may not want to be forced into group work, so these two assignment tracks allow them to choose the kinds of writing they want to commit to. So far, the majority of my students choose track A's team-based assignments with only a few choosing track B's individually-based assignments.

And so, the game pitch bridges either to a game proposal (more commonly known as a game design document in the game industry) for track A or a game research paper for track B. Students are asked to present and record their pitches onto Flip (a digital video discussion space often used by educators) for a low-stakes part of the assignment, as the rubric focuses mainly on their presentation design. The purpose of this presentation is two-fold. First, it provides a space to practice presenting before the in-class presentations required for the fourth major assignment, and for students on track A, it provides a digital space where students can watch each other's game pitch presentations to determine which pitches they are more interested in. From there, students on track A make a simple ranking list of these pitches, which I use to determine game design teams for the game proposal assignment.

Much of the game proposal and game research paper's rubric elements parallel their objectives. Both major assignments ask for a larger focus on research to better understand their game design or game topic, and both work to make an argument for a particular audience. While the game proposal asks for more of a focus on game design composition, the shared labor between team members as a part of collaborative writing enables them to work together to fill any potential gaps of any individual member to support each other as a team.

For students on Track A, a significant part of the game proposal is that after forming teams, the team members are required to work together to create a team contract that everyone signs and agrees to. I provide a template for them to work from and go over the questions that they need to answer, communication policies, non-participation policies, team availability schedule, and roles/tasks for each member. This helps to alleviate student concerns over grade impact if a member of the team does not contribute. I also facilitate draft updates to be submitted with annotations on individual member contributions to keep myself informed of team member contributions, along with check-ins with each member during workshop sessions.

I encourage students on track B to meet during team meetings/workshops to support each other, despite choosing individual writing assignments as part of their track. Small group and class discussions encourage students to foster a class community, which in turn enables them to more easily turn to each other for feedback and advice for the game research paper. This participation also helps students to more easily fit into teams and actively discuss the team contract, and their desired roles/tasks, and to collaborate on the team game design. Also, while the student who designed the original pitch of the game designs leans more into a leadership role, their authority in the teams, so far in my classes, has always made room for a more collaborative design and composition.

Collaboration is a significant part of this assignment as Andrea Lunsford (1991) argues:

> collaboration aids in problem-finding & solving, fosters interdisciplinary thinking, guides to more critical thinking, helps in understanding others, leads to higher achievement, and encourages active learning. Providing this kind of environment enables students to further develop the skills composition instructors are looking for (pp. 5-6).

Overall, the game pitch is the most direct bridge to the game proposal. Imagine that a member's pitch has been accepted for development and now a team must detail out their design so that the game is ready to be made. I explain that this is an actual step of the game development process called pre-production where the game design is made before actual production begins. Part of the scaffolding for this project is showcasing the team's processes, research, roles, and the purpose of the game proposal. This proposal, like the game pitch, works for two audiences: their peers (so that they are on the same page regarding the design process and progress) and their instructor (who functions as the project manager of the teams in the classroom, facilitating their process to ensure success).

On the other hand, the game think piece is the most direct bridge to the game research paper. I explain to students how the game research paper is a more academic and heavily-researched version of the game think piece. They must adhere to citation and formatting styles (APA or MLA) and use more sources to support their arguments. I have them begin with a complex research question to inform their thesis and stance on the topic and find their evidence. I also explain that the sources they research may differ from more traditional research papers, encouraging them to consider game magazine articles, game developer interviews, gaming community spaces, and the comment sections of videos on games to find the differing perspectives on the game topics they are interested in. I also encourage them to consider the game design aspects that they have learned throughout the course to bring in the research and points that they are making.

The fourth major assignment is either the game portfolio for students on track A or the game web resource for students on track B. The game portfolio builds upon the game proposal assignment by asking each member of a team to develop a specific kind of asset for their game design. These assets are chosen by each individual and are varied: sound/music/voice, concept art of characters/environments, dialogue scripts/character bios/story writing, level design/flowcharts, and screenshots/mockups of the user interface (the menus, interactable visual, and visual information provided while playing a game).

This assignment focuses on practice and play over a high-stakes final product, using the last weeks of the course to practice the production phase of the game design process. This helps to illustrate the practical use of design and the concept of transfer. Students can also see how managing a team project and collaboratively composing can result in tangible results. For the final exam, I have students present their individual assets to showcase the process of building their game design and the rhetorical choices in creating assets. This enables them to present their efforts and share what they have learned and created with the classroom community.

The game web resource also has a presentation aspect where they showcase what they've learned through their research about games, talk through their rhetorical choices in creating their game web resource, and share what they have worked on in the semester. The game web resource asks students to create a multimodal resource for a target audience that builds on the work and research they have done on a previous assignment, including the game think piece, game pitch, or game research paper. This gives students agency in deciding which prior major assignment focus will work best for their game web resource. They are given several formats they can work in, including blogs, social media posts/stories, videos, presentations, infographics, syllabi/magazines, and podcasts. They are also free to discuss other ideas outside the examples I present in the assignment sheet.

Discussion/Implications

Throughout the course, student responses are constructive and overall positive. To ensure understanding and provide a safe space for students to reflect on their process and progress in the course (along with any personal disclosures), I have students complete a low-stakes bi-weekly reflective journal. Within these journals, they reflect on being able to transfer understandings of rhetorical concepts of purpose and audience to other kinds of media and writing. They also write about learning about the potential of digital games and how their knowledge of game design aspects grew throughout the semester, along with a more nuanced understanding of what games were capable of. They discuss building important skills such as project management and research through the coursework. With these reflections, it became clearer to me that the same student learning outcomes and course objectives of traditional composition courses can be done with the theme of game design and development. Students also discuss in-class how different the classroom environment and expectations are from their other courses and express relief and joy in being in such a classroom.

Finally, they write about how the activities involving critical analysis of games led them to better develop their writing for game writing genres. I usually choose indie games that showcase aspects of games that are not typically represented in more familiar and mainstream games for these analysis activities. For example, one of these games that consistently engages students to participate in problem-solving is *Baba is You*. This game utilizes aspects of game design within its visuals and game mechanics. The game uses words within phrases to affect the gameplay and establish its rules. You play as "BABA," a small sheep-like creature, established by the phrase "BABA IS YOU" as a visual on the screen. And for an example of the gameplay, one phrase consists of "WALL," "IS," and "STOP." As a result, the player through the avatar of Baba is not able to move through or past the wall visuals. However, by using Baba to push the word "STOP" away from the phrase, the wall no longer restricts Baba's movement.

Game design uses this same kind of logic when designing its rules but usually not within the gameplay itself and so transparently to players. In this sense, the game enables students to become game designers through its gameplay. This also ties into digital games' strength of engagement that allows them to flourish and be enjoyed by many in the present day, particularly creative indie games like *Baba Is You*.

Students also write about how our collaborative community works well to support their learning in the classroom. While I was happy to answer students' questions when they raised their hands or came up to me during workshop time, students also asked their peers for help, and at times during my instructor check-ins, my students and I problem-solved together to help answer concerns and questions. And, particularly with the team projects of the game proposal and game portfolio, students are eager each class day to get together with their team members and discuss their creative designs and thoughts and problem-solve together to make rhetorical decisions as a team. At the end of the course, they were excited to see the end results of their collaborative, multimodal writing efforts and communicated their enjoyment of the course and the learning it helped to facilitate.

The course is not without some issues, though I mentioned how I addressed a couple of these earlier. I designed the course using Google Docs and Canvas. Students wrote in their journals that they enjoyed the collaborative note-taking activities and the daily agendas that I provide through Google Docs, but some students had trouble sharing in Google Docs, even throughout the semester. I did provide a worksheet to have them build a shared folder and provided individual support with this issue, but some students continue to struggle with this (particularly in my Spring 2023 course). While I'm not sure why my students in this semester's course had more trouble, it's important to consider that not all students know how to use digital tools, and time is needed to help with understanding Google Docs. Overall, Google Docs/folders works well for me and the students to work together, particularly for each other in peer review workshops and for me in better observing the growth of their drafts and writing, so I think it is worth keeping as the course's organizational structure.

Conclusion

Digital games are still stigmatized as violent in mainstream media, and at best, their value is only seen as entertainment. As a consumer and player of games for many years, I've always chosen games that spoke to me through their stories, characters, mechanics, and other multimodal aspects. And as years have progressed, games now tackle important issues and provide spaces for players to be heard and represented. While some composition instructors may hold resistance towards digital games and lack of awareness of their potential in the composition classroom (Alexander, 2009; Custer, 2013), my course design can bring awareness of their pedagogical potential and encourage other composition instructors to use digital games in the composition classroom, to develop teaching and literary experiences that are more accessible, dynamic, and creative. I also hope that it functions as a model resource for instructors interested in engaging students in creative ways and in developing their own writing courses based on digital game design and development.

In teaching such a course, I have a few suggestions. First, I recommend that composition instructors begin from their own familiarity and experiences with games. While I have a background of several years playing a variety of game genres, there are still genres I am more familiar with and ones that I'm less familiar with. Start with where you are comfortable and know that you can (and should) rely on your students to help fill in any gaps in your game knowledge background as you and your students form a community to collaborate and approach game design discourse.

In addition, writing instructors probably want to consider their classroom space and available technology. I requested specific classrooms that would have the technology to enable students to be able to play digital games in the classroom. I also noticed that while the classroom I used for my Fall 2022 course had more advanced technology available to use, the classroom I used for my Spring 2023 course was a bit smaller and allowed for easier communication across the space thus encouraging more classroom community-building as a result. Depending on your institution, you may be able to access games and technology from the institution itself or through institutional funding to help facilitate your course.

Finally, I strongly encourage composition instructors who are hesitant to fully take on a game design-themed composition course to at least explore course design aspects that they are interested in and implement them in their writing course. Also, to avoid shallow gamification, use what I have provided but also build upon it with your own research. Even if you only take a small step into this course design, digital game design can bring so much to your writing classroom through building community, creating alternative and more equitable spaces, encouraging collaborative writing, addressing multimodal literacy & digital rhetorical analysis, and increasing student engagement.

References

Alexander, J. (2009). Gaming, student literacies, and the composition classroom: Some possibilities for transformation." *College Composition and Communication, 61*(1), 35-63.

Ballentine, B. D. (2015, September). Textual adventures: Writing and game development in the undergraduate classroom. *Computers and Composition, 37*, 31-43. *Science Direct,* https://doi.org/10.1016/j.compcom.2015.06.003

Colby, R. S. (2017, January 10). Game-based pedagogy in the writing classroom. *Computers and Composition, 43*, 55-72. *Science Direct,* https://doi.org/10.1016/j.compcom.2016.11.002

Custer, J. (2013). *Play and praxis: Exploring the implication of videogame-infused pedagogy in the composition classroom* (Publication no. 1448514480) [Master's thesis, The Florida State University]. ProQuest Dissertations & Theses Global.

Gee, J. P. (2003). *What video games have to teach us about learning and literacy.* Palgrave Macmillan.

Juul, J. (2003). *The game, the player, the world: Looking for a heart of gameness.* Jesper Juul. https://www.jesperjuul.net/text/gameplayerworld/

Lunsford, A. (1991). Collaboration, control, and the idea of a writing center. *The Writing Center Journal, 12*(1), 3-10. https://www.jstor.org/stable/43441887

McGunnigle, C. (2023). Introduction. In C. McGunnigle (Ed.), *Gamification in the RhetComp curriculum* (pp. xii -xiix). Vernon Art and Science Inc.

Robison, A. J. (2008). The design is the game: Writing games, teaching writing. *Computers and Composition, 25*, 359-370. *Science Direct,* https://doi.org/10.1016/j.compcom.2008.04.006

Slentz, J. E., Kondrlik, K. E., & Lyons-McFarland, M. (2017). Spies like us: Gamifying the composition classroom and breaking the academic code. *Composition Studies, 45*(2), 187-209. https://www.jstor.org/stable/26402790

Appendix A
Example Game Pitch

ONE WEEKEND

By Lia Schuermann

"Can you find the words to fix what's breaking?"

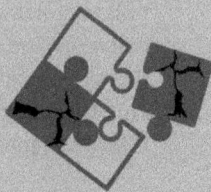

GAME OVERVIEW

One Weekend is a 2D narrative adventure game focused on the romantic relationship between two people who are struggling to communicate with each other.

The game is set in a small apartment and spans one weekend where the player makes choices that impact the characters' relationship. It'll be planned for PC due to my familiarity with the platform, but it can be potentially made for other platforms as well.

HEALING

This game seeks to have players play through an aspect of relationships not often discussed in games, how to heal and communicate. Games like these showcase this as they help their audiences "find a window into feelings or situations that they didn't understand before," as Litchford, Vice-President of independent game developer Deck Nine Games, states (as cited in Robertson, 2016, para. 13).

MENTAL ILLNESS

This game will also discuss mental illness as one of the characters suffers from past trauma. The player will at first not be told this directly at first, but through playing the game enough will reveal this and help them understand their partner.

Meagan Turner, a certified therapists says "Being able to recognize your partner's symptoms can help both of you heal from PTSD and improve your relationship. Important considerations for you to discuss with your partner... the triggers that impact them, and what helps them feel calm and safe. If your partner's changes go unaddressed, your relationship might become confusing, hurtful, and difficult to navigate together."

STORY

The story begins with two characters in a romantic relationship but on the verge of collapse. Miscommunication and misunderstandings, especially with mental illness, have led them to this one weekend, where their relationship may take a turn toward healing or to destruction.

Also, having done research on trauma narratives in digital, I feel prepared to represent trauma well in this narrative through my experience and knowledge.

POSSIBILITY

This story also illustrates the possibility for healing and successful relationships for those with mental illness or those in relationships with someone with mental illness.

Turner explains that "while dating someone with PTSD can be difficult, there are ways your relationship can be improved. Some of these include not minimizing their trauma, keeping things in perspective, encouraging your partner to seek treatment, accepting that trauma cannot be undone, becoming familiar with your partner's triggers, communicating your needs, and practicing self-care."

CHOICE & ENDINGS

Similar to the *Life is Strange* series, a game franchise that emphasizes the short and long-term effects of the choices you make, a large theme of the story will be on the choices you make affecting the ending you receive.

And similar to real relationships and life experiences, the player is not likely to ensure the relationship's success on the first playthrough. However, players will be able to replay the game and with more insight each time, helping them work to help the characters with their relationship and communication.

INTERACTION

The player will interact with the world by controlling one of the characters in the apartment and making everyday life choices such as washing dishes or deciding what to eat for dinner.

These choices will trigger conversation with the other character and choices can be made that vary with impact and the player will learn more about the characters and their relationship.

ART STYLE

This game will use a hand-drawn art style to focus on expression on character's facial and body language.

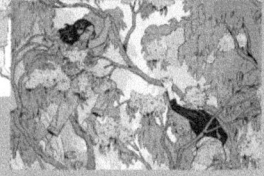

This will enhance immersion and the believability of the personalities and emotions of the characters.

ART STYLE

This hand-drawn art style will also enhance the believability of the setting and background by looking lived-in and detailed

This will also enhance immersion and encourage exploration of the setting as enables unique designs for each background detail.

AUDIENCE

This game targets adults who want to play meaningful stories with believable characters that tackle emotional challenges.

Game franchises like *Telltale Games* and *Life is Strange* showcase these narratives. Steve Allison, Senior Vice President of Publishing at Telltale Games, explains that these games are successful because "people love narrative. It's what drives TV, books and film and it's what drives our products. We make interactive scripted entertainment that works on devices that have large 17-35 year old audiences and we seek to work on franchises that those people are passionate about" (qtd. in Wong).

INSPIRATION

Drawing from *Twelve Minutes*'s repeat cycle of twelve in-game minutes where the player's choices change the story and ending the player.

Drawing from *Life is Strange: Before the Storm*'s focus on two primary characters whose story focuses on their relationship and how they communicate to heal from their issues.

WORKS CONSULTED

- Milledge, Sas. "'Mamo' Character Design." *Sas Milledge*, n.d., www.sasmilledge.com/character-design.
- Shutterstock. "Trauma and PTSD." 2019, www.counselling-directory.org.uk/memberarticles/trauma-and-ptsd-how-to-get-help-without-talking-about-it.
- Tan, Alben. "Community Study Room F." *Artstation*, 2020, www.artstation.com/artwork/nYwK2E.
- Turner, Meagan. "PTSD & Relationships: Supporting a Partner With PTSD." 18 Oct. 2022, www.choosingtherapy.com/ptsd-and-relationships/.
- *Twelve Minutes*. Annapurna Interactive, 2021.
- weem. "Character Designs 2009." *Deviantart*, 4 Oct. 2009, www.deviantart.com/weem/art/Character-Designs-2009-139231851.
- Wong, Steven. "The Telltale Games Method for Success." *a.list*, 15 Dec. 2015, www.alistdaily.com/strategy/the-telltale-games-method-for-success/.

WORKS CONSULTED

- bro.vector. "Tangled thread with heart between sad couple in stress, bad communication of man and woman flat vector." *freepik*, n.d., www.freepik.com/premium-vector/tangled-thread-with-heart-sad-couple-stress-bad-communication-man-woman-flat-vector-illustration-relationship-love-conflict-concept-banner-website-design-landing-web-page_20401277.htm.
- feodora52. "Marriage, relationship problems concept." *123rf*, n.d., www.123rf.com/photo_117562944_marriage-relationship-problems-concept-vector-of-a-couple-man-and-woman-standing-at-the-edge-of-the-.html?vti=niqoob2ddk0sbdvspv-1-1.
- ldi8t. "toyhouse." *Deviantart*, 13 May 2019, www.deviantart.com/ldi8t/art/toyhouse-purge-clearout-lf-art-trades-797511027.
- *Life is Strange: Before the Storm*. PS4 version, Square Enix, 2017.

Chapter 7

Teaching Intersectionality and Using Podcasts: A Discussion of Student Responses

Laura Dumin
University of Central Oklahoma

Abstract: Dumin focuses on using podcasts, TV shows, and articles to teach about intersectionality and DEI topics. Students had the opportunity to explore the American Dream and what college education can do for social mobility, while also exploring their own identities and how they fit into their communities.

Keywords: Podcasts; television; DEI; first-year composition; intersectionality

***

Introduction

For over a decade, I've been using a game project to teach research, development, and workplace writing in technical writing classes. Both Simmons and Schuermann (this book) discuss references and benefits of using games for teaching purposes, so I will not belabor the point here. Through teaching the game project, which went from a three-page assignment sheet with vague instructions to a 23-page assignment sheet with milestones and thought-out checkpoints, I became more comfortable with using assignments beyond just essays. About seven years ago, I was introduced to transformative learning (TL) and how Jack Mezirow views teaching students in ways that will change their perspectives somehow (see Brinson, 2021 for a brief overview). Because of Mezirow's influence, I began adding reflections to each of my projects and, a few years later, when I was introduced to the field of Scholarship of Teaching and Learning (SoTL) (Center for Engaged Learning, 2023), I began to look for ways to continue changing up my teaching and assignments to stay relevant and remain interesting for students. To that end, a few years ago, I decided to take a leap and use podcasts to introduce students to concepts of diversity, equity, and inclusion

(DEI) in a less threatening and more engaging manner by having students read about who goes to college, how that impacts social mobility, and how they see themselves fitting into different categories and groups. This chapter will focus on that course, student reactions, and the lessons learned.

Overview of the Project

As we see DEI (Diversity, Equity, and Inclusion) topics having more of a place in our culture, it makes sense to find ways to bring those topics into the classroom, if we can. Many states are making these discussions harder to have, and even taking steps to legislate what can and can't be taught (Bryant & Appleby, 2023). The writing classroom can be a safe space for students to begin discussing some of these deeper topics and to begin critical thinking lessons around both topics of DEI and why legislators might want to keep students from learning certain aspects of American history. I have found that each time I teach DEI topics, students are overwhelmingly appreciative of the opportunity to learn new things; they are also frustrated at not having been exposed to the information earlier in their academic lives. Given the positive reception to these types of assignments, I continue to look for ways to give students a variety of perspectives that they might not have heard before.

I have experimented with a few ways to accomplish this. In 2022, one of my first-year English Composition courses (a course based on teaching students to find their voices and write on various topics) used podcasts, a TV show, and a few articles to help students better understand both social mobility through college attendance and the concept of intersectionality. There were a few reasons that I wanted to use podcasts as part of this assignment: 1) the works can be more timely than waiting for peer-reviewed articles to be published; 2) low-cost/no-cost barriers for students to access the works; 3) students can choose whether to listen as they do something else, listen intently, listen quickly by changing up the playing speed, or even read the transcripts rather than listen, 4) students can hear reporters and the people involved in the stories speak in their own voices, which can bring more meaning and depth to the story, and 5) podcasts may have language that is easier to access and understand than peer-reviewed academic writing.

As for the topic of the course, reading about intersectionality, starting with Kimberlé Crenshaw's (1989) work on black women and the legal system, and moving through to more recent discussions of intersectionality and teaching (see essays within Kim Case's 2013 book *Deconstructing Privilege*), made me think about how we approach, in our classrooms, discussions of diversity, inclusion, and understanding of others. With the passage of bills like Oklahoma HB 1775, which limits discussions of eight concepts around race and gender in a variety of education-related spaces (Korth, 2022), our students are possibly going to be coming to us with a lesser understanding of how diversity has impacted American History, our current laws, and our societal norms. To begin combatting that concern, I designed a few Institutional Review Board [IRB]-approved studies using pre- and post-reflections with an eye toward the transformative experience. This has been well-received by students and has been an effective way to discuss diversity topics while also helping students to better understand their own positions within society.

For the purposes of this piece, the word "text" will be used to mean any of the items that we consumed, be that TV show, podcast, or article.

Intersectionality: What Is It?

The concept of intersectionality describes the ways in which systems of inequality based on gender, race, ethnicity, sexual orientation, gender identity, disability, class and other forms of discrimination "intersect" to create unique dynamics and effects. For example, when a Muslim woman wearing the Hijab is being discriminated, it would be impossible to dissociate her female* from her Muslim identity and to isolate the dimension(s) causing her discrimination. (Center for Intersectional Justice, n.d.)

When I hear the word "intersection," I think first of a plus sign, a standard four-way stop. But the reality is that all of us occupy more than just 2 or 3 spaces. Not all those spaces are equally occupied, leading to more of a star shape with lines that might not all be straight or even the same length (See Fig 7.1). It can be hard for many people in privileged spaces to realize all the spaces that they occupy, especially the invisible spaces like whiteness, heterosexuality, or the middle class (Daniels, 2021). It is the nuances of the invisible spaces along with the more visible ones like skin color, gender, sexuality, and physical/mental ability that really interest me. That is where I like to invest my teaching and discussions.

Figure 7.1. Intersectionality: Perception versus reality

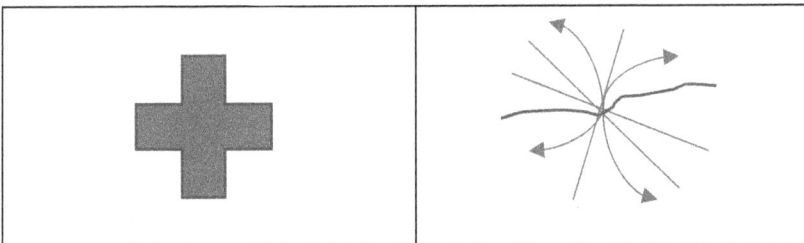

For college students, especially ones in their first year, these nuances may be hard to grasp. We had a whole generation of students who were taught that being

"color-blind" was the way to be, or who have been told not to point, stare at, or ask questions about people with different abilities or who are in non-heteronormative relationships. We have, effectively, seen society try to silence these differences in the name of getting along. But by silencing the differences or making the differences into boogeymen in the dark, we have compressed people into caricatures of their real selves, allowing only certain differences to "count."

It is in these nuances that I find teaching to be most interesting. Students appreciate the opportunity to look at people as more than just their race, gender, socio-economic class, etc., and to hear voices that discuss experiences outside of their own. By focusing on the nuances and spaces between categories or labels, teachers can bring deeper learning and understanding to their classrooms.

Who is More Oppressed

As I read through some of the mid-2000s literature, I noticed this idea of "who is more oppressed" coming up. Purdie-Vaughns and Eibach (2008) look at this idea and at some of the other literature that argues for one theory or another. It struck me as odd, almost 15 years later, that the "scorekeeping" method gained so much traction. Perhaps that is one of the bigger problems with intersectionality—historically marginalized groups must be willing to acknowledge that others, in both historically marginalized and privileged groups, can also be hurt in similar ways. No one group has a lock on the "most marginalized." And it can be hard for different groups to acknowledge the ways in which societal pain can be inflicted on other out-groups aside from their own. It can also be hard for groups such as white women, who face gender-bias, to see how adding race, socio-economic class, or sexual identity to the bias could also be problematic. Or when white men who have been marginalized because of their socio-economic class or education level have trouble sympathizing with black men from higher socio-economic classes. We can easily get caught up in our own frustrations and lose sight of how others can also be marginalized.

While I am glad to see that Purdie-Vaughns and Eibach (2008) push back against the score-keeping method of marginalization to an extent, arguing that certain intersections (such as Black, female, AND lesbian) become invisible rather than multiply marginalized, it is worth keeping the score-keeping concept in mind as we move into the classroom. Our own students may engage in this sort of behavior and thinking, simply because they have not been trained to see through the eyes of other groups. One of our jobs in teaching intersectionality, then, becomes the effort to show different sets of marginalized voices, not to show that one is worse off than another, but to show that different groups can be marginalized in different ways, and this is all a problem to be reckoned with.

Coalitional Subjectivity

Griffin and Chávez (2012) bring in Carrillo Rowe's discussion of coalitional subjectivities where "alliances and belongings are built across power lines so that privileged and oppressed people learn to belong to one another and to learn from one another about the nature of power and the possibility of social change" (p. 11). In this way, people learn to want to belong to these alliances because they bring about a richer and fuller understanding of other people and their needs and identities. Griffin and Chávez note that Rowe discusses the concern of white women being left out of intersectionality, however, this is a space where "white, straight, middle-class feminists can develop" (p. 11) an understanding of both oppression and privilege and their place in this system.

How to Use These Concepts in the Classroom

So where does the idea of intersectionality come into play? Griffin and Chávez (2012) say "an intersectional approach could help [scholars] articulate the ways that politics, social norms, and personal histories lay the foundation for...discourse" (p. 18). Using intersectionality as a lens for discussing readings allows us to embrace conceptual messiness and give voice to nuances of identities, the ways that identities can be both stable and organic, and the roles that communication plays in stability and fluidity" (Shanara Rose Reid-Brinkley, as quoted in Griffin & Chávez, 2012, p. 18). To continue this idea: "an intersection[al] approach would prompt [scholars] to attend to the many aspects of power and privilege...and how communication fostered, created, organized, helped maneuver through, silenced, and gave voice to that presence or absence" (Griffin & Chávez, 2012, p. 18). This article, plus the ones in Kim Case's book *Intersectional Pedagogy* ring true for how I teach and reminded me of what I keep coming back to in my classrooms—nuances; the whole person; how all of who we are impacts everything from how we interact with the world to how we perceive the world.

Griffin and Chávez (2012) discuss how different authors in their book are using intersectional theory in the classroom, listing a set of example questions to use as we talk to our students about the voices that are present in the classroom, 2 of which get at what I teach and why (pp. 18-19):

- "which identities are said to 'belong'...and why, and how what is said comes to be 'true'"
- "which identities are safe on our streets, in our cars, in public, and in our homes, why that safety is present, or not, the discourses that sustain this safety or lack of it, and why *safety, home, legal, right, true,* and *belong* are even states of being that can be granted and withdrawn"

These identities that we have and where we feel that we best fit in are two of the big issues that I often come back to.

My Classroom

For this current project on intersectionality, I had students reflect on their own identities, as well as the power that these identities give them or take away from them. We used an episode of the *Simpsons* to discuss the American Dream, a response to that episode from *Planet Money*, some discussions from *Freakonomics* about college and social mobility, and finally a more traditional discussion of privilege with Peggy McIntosh's (1989) article "White Privilege: Unpacking the Invisible Knapsack" (as shown in Appendix A) and a look at why classroom activities such as the privilege walk are problematic. Students responded to semester pre- and post-reflection prompts about power and identity and wrote reflections about each piece along the way.

The goal was to have students see how their own understanding of identity, power, privilege, and society have either shifted or solidified through listening to podcasts and reading articles about current issues in education and then discussing the topics and their implications in class.

The Project

Pre-reflections

I started the semester with 20 students, 18 of whom filled out pre-reflections, although not everyone gave answers to each question, and 13 of whom allowed their responses to be used in the study. I like to use pre-reflections to start my projects because it gives me a sense of where my students are starting from, and it gives all of us a chance to see growth, changes, solidifying of ideas, transformations in thinking and understanding, etc. (Mezirow et al., 2009). It can be hard to look back at ourselves over the course of a semester if we don't have a place to start from.

Question 1 asked students to identify themselves. Thirteen of the students answered these questions.

---

1. Each of us has different identities that we either give to ourselves or have placed upon us.
   a. Please list all of the different spaces and identities that you occupy.
   b. Please discuss how you see each of these identities impacting your life.

I tend to be purposefully vague so that students can answer as they see fit. While this leads to a wide, and sometimes interesting, set of descriptors, it also gives students the freedom to think about how they identify without me putting any limits on those answers.

Of the 13 student responses discussed here, with some of the same students indicating multiples within a category (sexuality and place within the family), we see that

- 5 indicated gender
- 8 indicated ethnicity
- 5 indicated economic status
- 6 indicated sexuality
- 3 indicated religion (all Christian)
- 2 indicated disability
- 7 indicated place within the family

Other identifiers, such as nerd, athlete, introvert, etc. showed up much less frequently. It is interesting to see how students view themselves and how they categorize the importance of different identifiers in their lives. I built a word cloud (Figure 7.2) from their responses because I like being able to see all the answers in a visual. This helps to see the variation in the answers.

Figure 7.2. Word Cloud of Identities

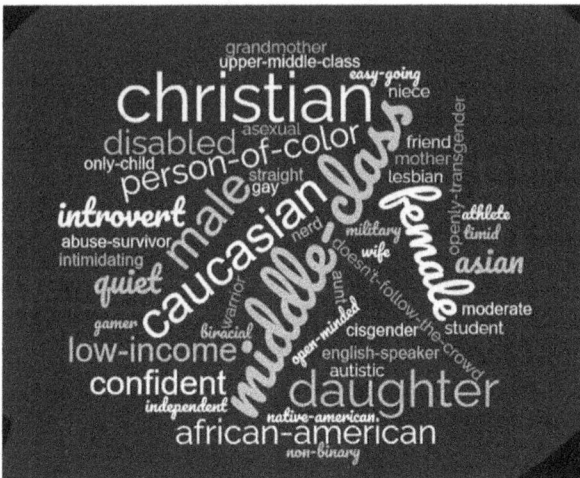

Generated using: https://www.wordclouds.com/

One student who identified as Christian, English-speaking, middle-class, moderate, male, and Caucasian was a bit more aware of the places where his identity impacted his daily life noting:

> Being a male enables me to be less scared (less in danger) when out and about by myself, day and night. .... I think being white can enable you to get better treatment from law enforcement, ... I can expect to be treated with a bit more empathy than those of non-white color. (Student 1.)

He was much more self-aware than many of the students at the beginning of the semester. Only a few of the males in the class noted their gender and only one of them really thought that it made much difference in their lived experience, as noted above. Same thing with being white or Caucasian. That was rarely mentioned and then those students who did mention it generally didn't see it as having much impact on their lives.

However, students who identified in ways that put them in the margins in some way were very much aware of how those identities shaped their lives. For example, one student who identified as white, autistic, openly-transgender, non-binary, lesbian, and disabled very clearly was able to see how their identities impacted their life, both positively and negatively.

> I have been called nasty names and even slurs for being a trans-autistic lesbian. I recently was harassed by frat boys for being disabled and walking with crutches. They were yelling at me that I 'better start running.' But I also have been impacted positively by being white. I sometimes get treated differently than people of color just because I look a little different. (Student 2)

Even with all the different challenges that the list of identities could present for them, they were also aware that being white gave them some breathing room and a positive identity.

Question 2 asked students to dig deeper into their identities and how they might gain privilege through any of those identities. Students had a slightly harder time with this question, which makes sense. For students who haven't been exposed to this idea before, the concept of what gives or takes away privilege can be hard to conceptualize.

2. We also each have ways that life is made easier or better for us, often because of these spaces that we occupy.

a. Please list the different ways that you have privilege. These can be smaller or larger. (Hint, look back at your identities and think about which ones give you access to places, information, money, power, etc.)

Please discuss how these privileges impact your life.

Four students did not respond in ways that were clearly answering these questions. For the other 9 students, socio-economic class, ethnicity, and gender were featured most often. Seven students discussed how their socio-economic status impacted them, with most of the comments being more favorable (Table 7.1). One student noted that because people around her thought that she had money, friends began to expect her to pay for everything when the group would go places. Eventually, she changed who she was spending time with and removed herself from the people that she felt were using her (Student 3). One student noted that their own socio-economic comfort made it harder to understand those who had less (Student 4).

The rest of the comments focused on positive things, mostly noting that money allowed them to have access to food, shelter, clothing, extra-curricular activities, and college.

Table 7.1. Socio-economic status and comments

Socio-economic class	Comment
Upper-middle class	
	Hard time understanding people without as much money
Middle-class	
	Money equals freedom to do things and go places
	Has food, housing, and clothing
	Financially stable; confused as a child by people who didn't have those things
	Can participate in activities and go to college
Lower-middle class	
	People expect her to pay for them to go places

	Access to college, healthcare, better job prospects
	Not as much access to newer things; has a comfortable life thanks to some scholarships and free or reduced healthcare costs

The next most often discussed identity was ethnicity and skin color (Table 7.2). Interestingly, everyone who commented on this part of their identity noted something positive about it. No one mentioned the negatives here, perhaps because they had mentioned those in question 1 and didn't want to come back to them again.

Table 7.2. Ethnicity/skin-color and comments

Ethnicity/skin-color	Comment
White	
	Possibly helped with the police report in a car crash, giving a more favorable report
	Cannot be discriminated against because of skin color. Not seen as suspicious. No need to be afraid of police. Not worried about being victim of hate crime based on race.
	General privilege because of skin color
Asian-American	
	Access to more networking groups and communities because they fit into multiple communities
Native-American	
	Access to land, healthcare, and scholarships for college

Gender was the third most mentioned identity (Table 7.3). Interestingly, the comment from the male was positive, while one of the female comments was neutral (that people offered to carry things for her—she wasn't sure how she felt about this) and one comment was negative in that she wished she were a male because of the extra privilege, and that she was tired of having to pay for period products when it wasn't her choice to have a period.

Table 7.3. Gender and comments

Ethnicity/skin-color	Comment
Male	
	Better outcomes in police interactions

	Better pay and promotions at work
Female	
	People offer to carry things
	Wishes she were male because they have more privilege

Question 3 asked students to think about their own experiences with being treated differently as well as their value judgments about the rightness/wrongness of how we experience that privilege.

---

3. Given what you have discussed above, think about a time or a few times when you have been treated differently (this can be better or worse) than friends or other people that you know because of these spaces that you occupy.

a. As you reflect on these times, think back: did you notice that you were being treated differently in the moment? Did you notice it later when you came back to it? Do you think that anyone else who was with you noticed? If it was a negative experience, did anyone intervene to try to change the situation? How did you feel after the moment was over?

b. Do you believe that there is a rightness or wrongness to the privilege that we might experience because of specific identities?

At this point, I was hoping to get students to think more deeply about privilege in their own lives because we all have identities that bring us some positives and we most likely have identities that bring us some negatives.

Students had a harder time with this question as well. There didn't seem to be much of a theme within the comments about where students felt like they had been treated differently. Some of them noted differences in how they were treated that were definitely based on identity and others noted differences that could simply be because they were unknown to the people in that situation. To illustrate this:

1) One student noted that they use crutches to get around. One of their friends used to ask why they wouldn't "just run," not realizing how ableist this sort of comment is. This student also noted that they used to be worried about reactions to using the handicap parking placard because they weren't using crutches full-time until recently. (Student 2)

2) Another student reflected on how his mother made dinner but served his friend a smaller portion. The student thought that this was racist

because it was a culturally traditional meal item. (Student 5) I'm not sure that I see it the same way. As a mother, I always serve other kids small portions because I'm never sure how much they will eat, and I don't want food to go to waste. This difference of perception is interesting though, because while I think the intention was about avoiding waste, that was not the perception from either the student or his friend.

As to the second part of the question, about the rightness or wrongness of having and using privilege, I wanted to get at that deeper question of how people feel about anyone using privilege to make things happen. Eleven people answered this piece of the question, with most students saying "both" (Table 7.4).

Table 7.4. Rightness and wrongness of using privilege

Right	Wrong	Both
1	3	7

I found it interesting that most students saw the nuances in when, where, and how privilege is used, and how the intent impacts the action. Of the 3 students who said it was only wrong, one of them discussed whiteness and the other two discussed general equity concerns. Interestingly, all three of these students had identities that put them at the margins in some way (disability, ethnicity, sexuality). It seems like many of our students are coming to us with more concerns about social justice and fairness in daily life, especially if they have experienced being pushed to the side at some point.

The Teaching

After the pre-reflections came in, we got into the readings and discussions on privilege, power, and social mobility for the semester. The main focus of the readings and podcasts was on who goes to college, where they go to college, and how college impacts their social mobility. This topic was inspired by several different places, including the *Simpsons* episode 728 "Poorhouse Rock," the *Planet Money* podcast on June 3, 2022, that responded to the *Simpsons* episode called "Homer Simpson vs. the economy," the *School Colors* podcasts from *Code Switch* in 2022, and three *Freakonomics* podcasts (500, 501, and 502) in 2022 about college attendance and social mobility. There were a few other texts in this unit looking at student loans and how where you live impacts what tools you have access to in elementary school, but these were the main ones before we ended with Peggy McIntosh's (1989) article "White Privilege: Unpacking the Invisible Knapsack."

My hope was that by discussing something that all the students had a stake in—college life—and attaching it to social mobility and privilege, most of the students would at least be interested in the readings and discussions. I also wanted them to dive into how our identities impact our daily lives and our long-term trajectories. Part of the reason for this lens is as a pushback to our current political climate. Students may hear ideas such as "hard work will get you everything," "pull yourself up by your bootstraps," "there is no such thing as structural racism—anyone can achieve whatever they strive to achieve," and so forth. In many cases, there is little reason for folks in the majority or invisible identities to interrogate these ideas, meaning that some students may take these concepts as truths. This effort to deny our history of systemically pushing certain groups of people to the edges while privileging other groups is being buried. Trying to hide real estate redlining, college acceptances, who qualified for loans, etc. leaves our students without a clear understanding of their past and how that influences the now and the future.

Post-reflections

I ended the semester with 18 students, 8 of whom filled out the post-reflections. Not everyone answered every question, but they all answered **questions 1 and 2**. These two questions gave students a chance to think about their own shifting and growth over half a semester of discussions. I wanted to have students think about their own growth so that it was evident to them how the information had changed or deepened their understanding of themselves and their own identities.

Those questions are looked at together here since many students answered them in interwoven discussions.

> 1. Look back at your original list of the spaces that you occupy. Have you added or changed any spaces from that original list? If so, which ones? (Please include both the original list and clearly indicate any modifications.)

> 2. Has your view of how you occupy spaces changed? If so, in what ways?

One student said

> The spaces I occupy are not different, but who I am in them is. Also, this class has made me want to do further research into these topics. Not only to become more knowledgeable on them but also to figure out what they mean to me personally. (Student 6)

I love that this student felt that she learned more about who she was through the course of the semester, even though much of what she noted revolved around sexuality and religion, which were not topics that we touched much on.

She notes:

> I used to think that privilege was inherently a negative thing, but now I
> see it as more of a neutral thing. I have come to the realization that it is
> almost inevitable, and understanding one's privilege can be advantageous.
> (Student 6)

This is one of those concepts that can be hard to grasp, and I was pleased to see
that she was realizing that everyone has privilege somewhere. Once we
understand that, we can better interact with the world by knowing how we fit
into it.

Another student noted that the only thing that hadn't really shifted in some
way for him was his identity as a Christian (Student 1). In thinking about the
spaces that he occupied/occupies, he said:

> I now see that some spaces are permanent and some are temporary;
> some are correlated with good things, others with bad, but most are
> correlated with both, depending on your perspective.

This response seems to go well with the previous one, in that privilege and
identity aren't necessarily good or bad but understanding them is still important.

One student noted that while her own spaces hadn't changed, her
understanding of how others perceive and occupy spaces had changed:

> I have not really changed anything in my life, yet I have, through listening
> to my classmates and reviewing our assignments, realized that some of
> my preconceived ideas were not completely [thorough]. Although I
> think my views have not changed, because I am still those things I was
> at the beginning of the class, it appears that I have a better understanding
> of what other students go through on their higher education paths.
> (Student 7)

Going on that same theme, another student said:

> My views on these spaces haven't necessarily changed all too much, but
> they have grown to include a bigger picture and to take into consideration
> how other people may experience these same spaces. (Student 8)

These two students were moved enough to comment on how reading about
other circumstances and hearing about their own classmates' experiences
allowed them to expand their own thinking about the topics. Part of why I like

the use of in-class discussions is that these discussions allow us to hear others from outside of our own bubbles. We know that talking with others can help us to better understand the world and ourselves (Betz, 2022; Place, 2017), and the classroom can be a safe space to explore identities and voices outside of our own. Giving students that place to question, discuss, and learn from others can help them on their journeys to understanding themselves better.

While all these students had different changes, they all experienced growth of some kind in how they understood identity and privilege. I think that we all hope, as we teach big concepts, that our students will take away something meaningful from the discussions, and I feel like these responses showed how that worked in this class.

For **Question 3**, I wanted to see if they had changed how they identified their occupied spaces.

> 3. Now think about your original list of places of power and privilege. Have you added or changed any places from that original list? If so, which ones? (Please include both the original list and clearly indicate any modifications.)

Most of the students indicated that they had learned to better understand themselves or their positions of power. One comment stood out to me because so often when we talk about race and identity, it seems like the focus is on everyone but white people. And I tried to get away from that:

> I knew that I had privilege being white but I didn't necessarily know in all the ways I was. I learned that I have privileges in ways I wouldn't even consider, like how cartoon characters are primarily white-coded. More examples would be whites mentioned more prevalently in educational history books, not having to worry about being questioned in public due to my skin color (police, bank, or in general spaces), posters, magazines, and commercials showing primarily my race, and not having to worry about being in a negative situation due to my race. (Student 4)

I appreciate how their understanding of their own privilege was clearer now, and that they were able to see many of the little places where being white is the default. That can be a big step for many students, to realize that society is designed to look and sound like the group with the loudest voice and most power.

Finally, I wanted to see if there were any other ideas that might have stood out to students in our readings and discussions. **Question 4** allowed students to discuss those other concepts not already mentioned.

> 4. Given what we have discussed this semester, how have your ideas about identity, power, and privilege shifted or solidified? What are some concepts that you learned about that have helped you as you shifted or solidified your ideas?

One student mentioned realizing that she wasn't just a random, generic person; she had more privilege than many others in the world (Student 8).

Another student really took to heart how her own ideas had shifted from discomfort about discussions of privilege to a willingness to talk about these things:

> At the start of this class, I didn't really want to talk about how I have white privilege because it was a sensitive topic, but I feel much more comfortable talking about it now; it's an important topic to discuss. I think that feeling of it being a sensitive topic was because my family members didn't really talk about it that much …. [I] learn[ed] a lot about how I'm privileged as well as how I'm at a disadvantage because I'm a woman. (Student 4)

One of the young men in my class discussed what he felt was most important to him:

> My views have solidified with respect to how power and privilege are not necessarily bad in all cases, … but my views have shifted in that I consider intersectionality and the privileged and underprivileged perspective to have the strong potential to be used in unproductive and even counterproductive ways. The concepts that contributed to this solidification and shiftification were intersectionality; systemic discrimination, including everything that reinforces prejudice and discrimination; and just a greater understanding of what prejudice and discrimination are. (Student 1)

One student who is in a mixed-race relationship noted how her ideas had shifted some because of the readings and discussion:

> It broadened my ideas and thoughts about what more my white privilege has allowed me to be able to do. Another discussion we had in class was that privilege does not always have to be bad. I had an idea of this already, but speaking in a class made the idea carry more weight. (Student 9)

I appreciate the learning that led to these reflections. All these students demonstrated that the readings and discussions had helped them to better understand some concepts of power and privilege, and helped many students feel more comfortable having these types of discussions.

One of the assignments that we discussed and critiqued, but did not perform, was the "Privilege Walk." I had conceptualized the semester as including this activity until I read a piece in *The Chronicle of Higher* Education by Len Gutkin (2021) that discussed why this type of activity was more harmful than helpful. Instead of completing the activity, we read about the problems with it and discussed that article.

> The privilege walk assignment expanded my knowledge of privilege, what it's like to have it, and how lack of it can affect people. It also encourages me to think about the different privileges I possess. (Student 10)

Most of the students noted in class that they had not thought about the damage that could be inflicted on participants who were left behind as the rest of the class moved forward. Or they discussed their own experiences with these sorts of activities and how awkward it had been for them, especially if they had the privilege and kept moving ahead.

The Takeaways

I wasn't sure how using podcasts was going to work, given that this was the first time I had brought them into a classroom in a large way. I learned that while many students felt like it was nice to listen to their homework while they were driving, at the gym, cooking dinner, etc., others were not thrilled at having to listen to long pieces. I get that not everyone will respond to different mediums of text presentation, but I appreciated that students could access these texts in ways that written-only texts may not be accessible. I also realize that their focus may fade in and out if they are listening and completing other tasks, but it seemed like students were coming to class more prepared than when they only had a written piece to work with. Overall, using podcasts in my classes is now something that I do on a regular basis when I want students to hear current ideas in the voices of the people being impacted by the issues.

The post-reflections along with the general class discussion left me feeling positive at the end of this unit. Even though the idea of digging deep into how our identities, both visible and invisible, impact our lived experiences was new to many of the students, almost everyone had a positive reaction to learning about these ideas. The pre- and post-reflections allowed students to see their own growth, shifting, and solidifying which may have lent to a more positive reaction to the material. I was also pleased that most students who had one major visible identity that was often used to describe them (such as race or physical disability) could also see other places where they might gain or lose privilege based on other parts of their identity.

The biggest lessons that I feel like students left with were:

1) We can talk about identity without it being a bad conversation

2) We all have positive identity traits that help us in different situations

3) Even people who appear outwardly to have only positive identity traits may also have places where they are viewed negatively because of other, less visible identities

4) Talking with others helps us to better understand the world and our places in it

Conclusion

If we want to aim for transformative classroom experiences for both our students and ourselves, we must be willing to talk about things that matter to them or frame our content in ways that allow them to see the information through different lenses. Using things like podcasts and TV shows can allow students to hear other voices, quite literally, discussing these topics. This can bring more understanding and depth to the topics and can allow students time to ponder the information more deeply. It is harder to skim through a podcast or TV show than it is to skim a reading.

It can be a challenge to step outside of our own identities and teach from other perspectives, especially when we are new to hearing those other voices ourselves. We must acknowledge our own privilege as instructors, or lack thereof, and acknowledge how our views and experiences have colored our lives and paths. While this can be difficult and sometimes painful, doing that preparatory work on ourselves can make it easier to have these conversations with students later. We need to let go of the neatness of individual identity boxes and help our students move beyond categories. Griffin and Chávez (2012) note that "[w]e can no longer pretend that we exist outside the web of complexity that makes us all raced, classed, gendered, sexed, and differently abled individuals who belong or don't belong to particular nation-states" (p. 20).

Jones and Wijeyesinghe (2011) note that there is concern about how to present identities to students, understanding that for learners who are just coming to these concepts, talking about all the identities at once can lead them to become confused or can cause them to misunderstand how some identities can help and some can hurt. They reference Luft (2009) who suggests starting with one identity concept, such as race or gender, helping students to understand the impact of that identity, and then moving on from there. While I can see the benefit of taking things slow with new learners, I can also see how this could still trap students into the boxed identity ideas, where our identities are separate instead of being intertwined. Given that most instructors will have, at most, 16 weeks to work with students, taking it slow may not give the learning impact that faculty are hoping for.

Jones and Wijeyesinghe (2011) suggest that one way to help students grapple with the concepts of intersectionality is for faculty to model their own struggles and places of power and privilege, or lack thereof (p. 17). I am a strong proponent of bringing in my own struggles with concepts to show students where I have gained knowledge, made missteps, and recovered from those missteps. I also believe that we should let students know, at least generally, where we are coming from so that they can be aware of how our identities influence how and what we see about the world. By modeling our own struggles and naming our own identities, we can help students see 1) a learning mindset and 2) how different identities interact to make a whole personality.

I plan to keep a unit like this in the future, just changing up the readings as needed to keep the content fresh and current. While our legislature continues to fight about what students should or shouldn't be allowed to learn, I keep receiving positive feedback for introducing students to concepts that are new to them or introducing old concepts in new ways. If multimodal content such as what was discussed here helps students to understand the material more deeply, that seems like a winning way of teaching difficult concepts.

Appendix A

This is the list of texts used for the project. Most, but not all of them, were podcasts.

Text used	Type
Bennett, J., Fry, R., & Kochhar, R. (2020, July 23). *Are you in the American middle class? Find out with our income calculator*. Pew Research Center. https://www.pewresearch.org/short-reads/2020/07/23/are-you-in-the-american-middle-class/	Website
Donaldson, S. (2022, May 2). *A nonprofit tried to re-enroll thousands of students who almost finished college. Here's how it went*. The Chronicle of Higher Education. https://www.chronicle.com/article/a-nonprofit-tried-to-re-enroll-thousands-of-students-who-almost-finished-college-heres-how-it-went?cid=at&source=&sourceid=&cid2=gen_login_refresh	Article
Freedman, M., Griffith, M. W., Shockley, S., Rubin, C. & Levinson, I. (Executive Producers). (2022, July 1). School colors episode 8: The only way out (No. 355). [Audio podcast episode]. In *Code Switch*. NPR. https://www.npr.org/2022/06/30/1109160606/school-colors-episode-8-the-only-way-out	Podcast
Gutkin, L. (2021, Dec 13). *The review: 'Privilege walks'; Scientology; Secularization*. The Chronicle of Higher Education. https://www.chronicle.com/newsletter/the	Article

-review/2021-12-13?utm_source=Iterable&utm_medium=email&utm_campaign=campaign_3360233_nl_Academe-Today_date_20211213&cid=at&sourc%E2%80%A6	
Lapinski, Z. (Executive Producer). (2022, Apr 20). What exactly is college for? (No. 500). [Audio podcast episode]. In *Freakonomics Radio*. Freakonomics Radio Network. https://freakonomics.com/podcast/what-exactly-is-college-for/	Podcast
Lapinski, Z. (Executive Producer). (2022, Apr 27). The university of impossible-to-get-into (No. 501). [Audio podcast episode]. In Freakonomics Radio. *Freakonomics Radio* Network. https://freakonomics.com/podcast/the-university-of-impossible-to-get-into/	Podcast
Long, T. (Writer), & Moeller, J. (Director). (2022, May 22). Poorhouse rock (Season 33, Episode 22) [TV series episode]. In A. Jean & M Selman (Executive Producers), *The Simpsons*. Gracie Films and 20th Television.	TV episode
Lu, A. (2022, May 3). *Why talk of student-debt cancellation is creating headaches for colleges*. The Chronicle of Higher Education. https://www.chronicle.com/article/why-talk-of-student-debt-cancellation-is-creating-headaches-for-colleges?cid=at&source=&sourceid=&cid2=gen_login_refresh	Article
McIntosh, P. (1989). "White privilege: Unpacking the invisible knapsack." In *Peace and Freedom*, July/August.	Article
Rubin, W. (Executive Producer). (2022, Apr 15). The student loan paaaaauuuuuse (No 1,528). [Audio podcast episode]. In *Planet Money*. NPR. https://www.npr.org/transcripts/1093113723	Podcast
Smith, S. V. & Hirsch, P. (Executive Producer). (2022, June 3). Homer Simpson vs. the economy (No. 1,542) [Audio podcast episode]. In *Planet Money*. NPR. https://www.npr.org/2022/06/02/1102751823/homer-simpson-vs-the-economy	Podcast

References

Betz, M. (2022, Sept 14). *What is self-awareness and why is it important?* BetterUp [blog]. https://www.betterup.com/blog/what-is-self-awareness

Brinson, S. (2021, May 14). *The 10 phases of Mezirow's transformational learning theory*. DIY Genius. https://www.diygenius.com/transformational-learning/

Bryant, J. and Appleby, C. (2023, May 1). *These states' anti-DEI legislation may impact higher education.* https://www.bestcolleges.com/news/anti-dei-legislation-tracker/

Case, K. (Ed.). (2013). *Deconstructing privilege: Teaching and learning as allies in the classroom.* Routledge.

Center for Engaged Learning. (2023). *What is SoTL?* Elon University. https://www.centerforengagedlearning.org/studying-engaged-learning/what-is-sotl/

Center for Intersectional Justice. (n.d.). *What is intersectionality?* https://www.intersectionaljustice.org/what-is-intersectionality

Crenshaw, K. (1989). Demarginalizing the intersection of race and sex: A black feminist critique of antidiscrimination doctrine, feminist theory, and antiracist politics. *University of Chicago Legal Forum, 1989*(1), 138-167. https://chicagounbound.uchicago.edu/uclf/vol1989/iss1/8

Daniels, J. (2021). *Nice white ladies: The truth about white supremacy, our role in it, and how we can help dismantle it.* Seal.

Griffin, C. L., & Chávez, K. R. (2012). Standing at the intersections of feminisms, intersectionality, and communication studies. In C. L. Griffin & K. R. Chávez (Eds.), *Feminist voices: Feminist practices in communication studies* (pp. 1-31). State University of New York Press.

Gutkin, L. (2021, Dec 13). The Review: 'Privilege Walks'; Scientology; Secularization. The Chronicle of Higher Education. https://www.chronicle.com/newsletter/the-review/2021-12-13?cid2=gen_login_refresh&cid=gen_sign_in

Jones, S. R., & Wijeyesinghe, C. L. (2011). The promises and challenges of teaching from an intersectional perspective: Core components and applied strategies. *New Directions for Teaching and Learning 125*, pp 11-20. https://doi.org/10.1002/tl.429

Korth, R. (2022, Sept 8*). FAQ: What we know about teaching since Oklahoma's so-called critical race theory ban went into effect.* State Impact Oklahoma. https://stateimpact.npr.org/oklahoma/2022/09/08/faq-what-we-know-about-teaching-since-oklahomas-so-called-critical-race-theory-ban-went-into-effect/

Luft, R. E. (2009). Intersectionality and the risk of flattening difference: Gender and race logics, and the strategic use of antiracist singularity. In M. T. Berger and K. Guidroz (eds.), *The Intersectional Approach: Transforming the Academy through Race, Class, & Gender.* The University of North Carolina Press.

Mezirow, J., Taylor, E. W., & associates. (2009). *Transformative learning in practice: Insights from community, workplace, and higher education.* Wiley. https://www.google.com/books/edition/Transformative_Learning_in_Practice/OcVhvLDB22MC?hl=en&gbpv=1&dq=jack+mezirow+transformative+learning&printsec=frontcover

Place, S. (2017, Aug 15). *The science of person perception: Why it's important and why most of us aren't good at it.* Cogito [blog]. https://cogitocorp.com/blog/science-of-person-perception/

Purdie-Vaughns, V., & Eibach, R. P. (2008). Intersectional invisibility: The distinctive advantages and disadvantages of multiple subordinate group identities. *Sex Roles 59*, pp 377-391. DOI: 10.1007/s11199-008-9424-4

College Classrooms, Beyond the Writing Classroom

Chapter 8

Video Games and Fantasy Medievalism in the Music History Classroom

Daniel Atwood

Northwestern University

Abstract: Atwood introduces us to the use of video games and movie music to help students relate to Medieval music and the history of the music. Little of the music of Medieval minstrels has survived, and students may not have heard much of the music outside of popular culture depictions, this can be a way to bring students back to the lessons and actively engage in learning the material.

Keywords: video games; movie music; history

*** *** ***

Introduction

To many students, the arcane history of medieval music may initially hold limited appeal, yet the wide success of medievalist fantasy in television, film, and video games in recent years illustrates the significant cultural cachet of this era in the popular imagination. By drawing on these medievalist media representations, instructors can spark student interest in the Middle Ages, while also exploring questions of medievalism, cultural production, and the interplay of historical representation and fantasy in popular culture. Rooted in the principles of culturally relevant pedagogy and engaged learning, this approach invites students to think about what "medieval" means in their own cultural experiences. In this essay, I describe how this approach can be fruitfully deployed in the context of the music classroom, drawing on my experience teaching undergraduate music appreciation courses at Northwestern University.

By incorporating musical examples from best-selling games such as *The Elder Scrolls: Skyrim* and *Dragon Age: Inquisition* into my unit on medieval music, I observed a significant increase in student engagement and discussion. Students were excited to compare these representations with historic iconography and what they had learned in their readings on medieval music and musical medievalism. In particular, we focused on representations of the archetypal character of the singing, lute-playing minstrel—a staple of popular medievalism for centuries, from Beckmesser's serenade in Wagner's *Die Meistersinger von Nürnberg* to the strumming rooster Alan-a-Dale in Disney's *Robin Hood*. By using a variety of learning materials respectively emphasizing historical musical practice and popular medievalist tropes, students gained insight both into the history of medieval music and the history of reimagining medieval music in modern popular culture. For example, students were eager to note that the bards of *Skyrim* sing songs about the region's political intrigues—and I was eager to point them to examples of historic ballad singers doing much the same thing. After the in-class discussion, students were given the assignment to write a journal entry reflecting on an example of their choosing from medievalist video games, film, or television. Students were provided a list of choices but encouraged to think of their own examples.

This project created a space of greater accessibility and cultural immediacy for the medieval music unit of my course. In addition to facilitating student learning about historical musical practice and the contemporary representation of historical eras, it also offered them the opportunity to develop tools for discussing music and representation in film and video games more broadly, including archetypal character tropes, musical stereotypes, and the interplay of visual, musical, and narrative elements in diegetic musical scenes. My experience with this exercise suggests that the incorporation of contemporary medievalist works into the medieval lesson plan—in music history as well as other fields—can drive student engagement in a way that traditionally-oriented lesson plans often fail to do. Further, it offers students the chance to reflect on the concept of "the medieval" in relation to the contemporary popular cultural paradigms that they might encounter in their everyday lives.

Goals and Rationale

As John Haines (2014) observed, far more people alive today "have seen a film based on the Middle Ages than have read a scholarly book on it or attended a historical performance concert" (p. xvi). The wide popularity of films, television series, and video games such as *The Hobbit* trilogy (2012-2014), *Game of Thrones* (2011-2019), and *The Elder Scrolls* (2011), respectively, demonstrate the thriving prevalence of medievalism across a variety of screen forms, especially in fantasy (notwithstanding notable historically-themed examples such as 2018's *Kingdom Come: Deliverance*, set in early fifteenth-century Bohemia). In terms of the soundtracks for such medievalist works, Haines argues that the "few fragments that survive for medieval music pale by comparison to all of the details that filmmakers are obliged to invent" (p. 158) —an invention that "follows a venerable tradition" of representing the Middle Ages through a consistent representational language of various musical, visual, and narrative tropes and signifiers. While Haines was writing about cinema, this representational legacy is also carried forward through video games, another medium wherein medieval fantasy thrives, as has been explored by James Cook (2020). While scholars such as Karen Cook (2018) have extended Haines's work into the domain of video games with her studies of plainchant in Halo and other games, there has been little published on the adoption of this work in teaching contexts.

Given the widespread cultural cachet of the genre, particularly in media often associated with youth culture, it merits attention in the classroom. Bailey (2012) has argued that a teacher's inclusion of videogame analysis in the classroom demonstrates to students "that their local knowledge [is] an important resource for learning" and "that popular culture has validity in school" (p. 50). Zancanella et al. (2000) have considered video games from an aesthetic and literary perspective "as texts worth serious consideration in classrooms," (p. 101) through, among other approaches, a study of the involved representational languages and depictions of social and historical conditions. They observed that classroom analysis of video games can help students make connections between previously studied material and the video game representations, and, in the process, "learn about themselves, others, and the culture that produces and plays them" (p. 101). These aspects are particularly valuable in the music classroom, given the lingering perception that music instruction in institutionalized settings is "decontextualized from [student's] realities," alien to their own experiences and desires (Barton, 2018, p. 67). And, as Walker (2001) has noted, a relevant music education must "deal in what a culture believes is music and how music functions within the culture" (p. 13), a prospect which certainly entails the study of musical representations in popular culture artifacts; in classrooms filled with Prensky's (2001) "digital natives," who have "spent their entire lives surrounded by and using computers, videogames [sic], … and all the other toys and tools of the digital age" (p. 1), video game studies offer considerable cultural relevancy, especially in contrast with the otherwise often arcane, mysterious and far-off domain of medieval music. The specific approach advocated in this chapter follows the case-based method for teaching music advocated by Sara Haefeli (2022), using one of Haines' (2014) archetypes as the theme.

While a lesson plan incorporating video game music could likely succeed with any of Haines' (2014) domains of medievalism—as Karen Cook's (2018) research on plainchant in the *Halo* series suggests—I find that the medieval minstrel serves as a highly effective choice, due to its especially wide currency in popular culture. Further, the abundance of video game representations of medieval minstrel music serves as a useful counterbalance to the striking absence of actual preserved minstrel music in the historical record. While the sacred plainchant of the Middle Ages has been reasonably well preserved in notation (though many mysteries remain about performance details), the same cannot be said for medieval secular music. As Haines noted, "the performance art of the minstrel was transmitted orally and never, as far as we know, written down" (p. 88) —and even for the comparatively more extensively documented music of the courtly, elite troubadours referenced by Haines, only about one-tenth as much music as poetry survives (Stevens et al., 2001). Those sources provide only the melody's text and pitches, without notated information about rhythm, meter, accompaniment, or manner of performance. In this sense, important details of the musical practice of both medieval minstrels and the troubadours and trouvères are historically elusive to us, although to differing extents. Both offer opportunities for students to learn about secular songs in the medieval period, as well as the reconstructive and speculative processes by which we come to apprehend them so many years later. A study of the music of the troubadours offers students the chance to engage with historic music notation in medieval sources as well as the modern performances of that music, and a study of video game representations of minstrels provides them the chance to explore the long-running representational tradition of imagining the Middle Ages in popular culture while engaging with familiar sources of a more immediately accessible cultural relevance. For these reasons—and based on my experiences teaching the material—I find that a lesson plan pairing historical troubadours (and modern musical interpretations) with medievalist representations of minstrels in fantasy media can be a highly effective unit for drawing out student interest and increasing engagement.

There is a good deal more flexibility and interplay between these two sides than it might initially appear; for different reasons, and to different audiences, both sides involve a significant degree of—to borrow a phrase from musicologist John Butt (2002) — "playing with history." A lesson plan incorporating this approach offers students a place to think across the boundaries of historical and fantasy representation to consider how, for example, historically-informed performers of troubadour music must still necessarily make significant conjectural musical impositions upon on the limited music notation in their thirteenth-century sources, or how newly-composed "medieval minstrel music" still often reaches to centuries-old tunes and tropes for inspiration. It invites them to make connections between and about the processes by which representations of medieval music reach our ears and eyes in the present, both in academic, historically-minded musical contexts and in the wider popular culture. More broadly, it offers students an opportunity to engage with the limitations, affordances, and imaginative possibilities surrounding the music of the past. With only modest effort, an instructor might modify this lesson plan to largely omit the troubadours and focus exclusively on the twentieth- and twenty-first-century medievalism of minstrel representations, depending on their course goals, but I find that pairing them affords a particularly fruitful range of questions and connections across centuries and contexts. That is, that the historical examples are not simply there to bolster the "medieval music history" bona fides of a music history course—as if lending legitimacy to the inclusion of popular modern examples— but rather that the interaction between both of these two modes actually produces a richer and more engaged learning experience than focusing on only one or the other, because of the additional parallels and contrasts it allows students to draw.

Lesson Plan

While there are many ways to approach the topics discussed thus far—medievalism, representations of minstrels on the screen, and historic medieval secular song—the class materials and lesson plan given in Figures 8.1 and 8.2 reflect the approach I take in teaching undergraduate music appreciation courses at Northwestern University. Figure 8.1 outlines the materials for pre-class distribution and in-class use, including readings as well as video and audio examples, while Figure 8.2 sketches a timeline for how those materials might be deployed across a one-hour and twenty-minute class session. The materials include listening examples and readings pertaining both to historic medieval songs and to twentieth-century medievalist minstrel tropes, which can be adapted in a variety of ways depending on particular course goals or instructor preferences. In my class, this lesson is presented as part of a larger chronological sequence on the history of Western art music which comprises approximately half of the course. The medieval music section also includes a class session on sacred music and developments in plainchant across the centuries, which precedes this one, ensuring the students have some initial familiarity with the music and notation of the era, and some of the challenges of its research, interpretation, and performance.

This lesson plan includes a moderate amount of pre-class reading and viewing material, with four pages on troubadours from a traditional music history textbook (Kamien's (2022) *Music: An Appreciation*), approximately four pages from the music encyclopedia *Grove Music Online* entry on minstrels (Gushee et al, 2013), and selected excerpts from Haines's (2014) chapter on the medieval minstrel in his book *Music in Films on the Middle Ages: Authenticity vs. Fantasy*. For my purposes, I found it effective to present students with a highly excerpted form of Haines's chapter, emphasizing the discussion of musical and representational language involved in depicting minstrels, while de-emphasizing his specific case studies of films from the early 1950s. The entire chapter can be made available as part of the online course components for students who wish to indulge further.

Figure 8.1. Class Materials

- Pre-Class Materials:
- o   Reading (~17 pages):
  - ▪   Kamien *Music: An Appreciation* (2022)
    - •   Part 2, Chapter 3: Secular Music in the Middle Ages (~4 pages)
  - ▪   Haines (2014) Excerpts (9 excerpted pages)
    - •   Preface Excerpt: xv-xvi (2 pages)
    - •   Chapter 5: "The Singing Minstrel" Excerpts: 88, 94, 95-96, 99, 110, 157-158 (~7 pages, highly excerpted)
    - •   Optional reading: Conclusion, 153-158
    - •   [Include whole chapter on Canvas for interested students]
  - ▪   "Minstrel" – Entry on minstrels in *Grove Music Online* (~4 pages)
    - •   2. Early History, 3. Minstrel Instruments and ensembles, 4. Minstrels' music, 5. The minstrel in society, 8. Conclusion
- o   Video viewing:
  - ▪   YouTube: "The Tale of Brave Sir Robin" https://www.youtube.com/watch?v=jYFefppqEtE
  - ▪   YouTube: "Robin Hood – Not in Nottingham" https://www.youtube.com/watch?v=c2dImprgiB8&
  - ▪   YouTube: "Beatriz de Dia: A chantar m'ér de çò qu'eu no volria": https://www.youtube.com/watch?v=m2B00v5pD3k

- In-class materials:
- ▪   Viewing/discussion: Original notation for "A chantar" from *Manuscrit du Roi*, Folio 204: https://gallica.bnf.fr/ark:/12148/btv1b84192440/f423.item
  - •   Accompanying audio: YouTube: "Beatriz de Dia: A chantar m'ér de çò qu'eu no volria" https://www.youtube.com/watch?v=5Zah4VWPiNE
  - •   Video: Skyrim Bard, https://www.youtube.com/watch?v=0dj7EVJ_mtA&t=1s
- ▪   Listening Comparison:
  - •   "Oh Grey Warden" from Dragon Age https://www.youtube.com/watch?v=Bqu5GyIH0BE
  - •   "Packington's Pound," 16th century broadside ballad, perf. Tartleton's Jig https://www.youtube.com/watch?v=-JwwYNWWN40
- ▪   Listening Comparison:
  - •   "Once We Were" from Dragon Age: Inquisition https://www.youtube.com/watch?v=7Ja3nxXGqn4
  - •   "South Wind," traditional Irish tune, perf. Archie Fisher https://www.youtube.com/watch?v=_H3HlT5pia0

On the online Canvas page for this lesson, I also include some pre-class viewing requirements. First, a modern, historically-informed rendition of the Occitan song "A chantar m'ér de çò qu'eu no volria" by the twelfth-century trobairitz (female troubadour) Beatriz de Dia; the students read about Beatriz and this song in the Kamien (2022) text, and this audio gives them a chance to have at least one interpretation of the music in their ears. Second, I include a pair of video examples of medieval minstrels in twentieth-century film to refresh the students on the imagery and sounds of minstrels in medievalism of previous generations: one from Disney's 1973 *Robin Hood*, and another from the 1975 *Monty Python and the Holy Grail*. Optionally, one might include more recent examples, such as Jaskier's "Toss a Coin to Your Witcher" in the 2019 season of Netflix's *The Witcher*; I opt to include screenshots (rather than video) of recent instances from *Game of Thrones* and *The Witcher* television series as supporting imagery, which students can quickly visually scan and be reminded (or made aware for the first time) of these popular recent cases. This online space can be a good place to include a variety of medieval minstrel, bard, or troubadour representations, spanning from medieval texts such as the thirteenth -century *Cantigas de Santa Maria* to more recent examples such as *Dungeons and Dragons* character manuals, Renaissance Fair musicians, or fantasy cinema. Students can be encouraged to submit familiar examples in advance of the class meeting (or asked to come to class with an example in mind), to be used in the class session to open discussion and analysis, giving students a more active role in building the content of the lesson. Alternatively (or additionally), they can be asked to provide and discuss their own examples in collaborative discussion board assignments to be completed after the class session. Either of these techniques can help increase students' active learning, by applying the ideas from the reading and class session through integration with their own experiences with popular media—key categories in Fink's (2013) taxonomy of significant learning (p. 90).

Figure 8.2. Lesson Plan for One Hour and Twenty Minute Class Session

- 25 minutes. Introduction to medieval secular song and troubadours.

- Historical background
- Listening exercise, "A chantar" with original manuscript notation.

- 10-15 minutes. Transitioning from troubadours to minstrels

- Compare and contrast; historical records, social positions, amount of preserved music, etc.
- Haines's minstrel and student examples.

- 10-15 minutes. *Skyrim* video example; group analysis and discussion.
- 15-20 minutes. *Dragon Age: Inquisition* listening exercises.

- 7-10 minutes. Listening exercise with "Oh, Grey Warden" and "Packington's Pound."
- 7-10 minutes. Listening exercise with "Once We Were" and "South Wind."

> - 10 minutes. Assignment details and open floor for discussion and questions about the day's materials.

Classroom Methods

I developed and taught this lesson for a music appreciation class of just under thirty students who met twice a week for sessions lasting one hour and twenty minutes. As a course for non-music majors, the class had students from a wide variety of disciplinary backgrounds, from engineering to journalism to computer science. Although there were no music majors in the class, around half of the students had some degree of musical training or performance experience; for example, one had performed a cello concerto in high school, another played in a punk rock band on the weekends, and another performed in one of the university's student-run acapella groups. On the other end of the spectrum, one or two students considered themselves patently unmusical—a notion of which I hoped to relieve them at least slightly by the course's end. With such a wide range of disciplinary and musical backgrounds, I was especially attuned to the challenges and necessity of engaging all the students, without boring the musicians or speaking in unfamiliar technical jargon to everyone else. At the same time, recognizing the opportunity that such a breadth of perspectives offers for the group learning experience, I encouraged the students to take advantage of their participation in such a wide-ranging cohort, learning from one another by bringing their unique backgrounds and disciplinary knowledge to the class discussions.

To begin the troubadour/minstrel class session, I like to have a relevant musical example—Beatriz de Dia's "A chantar" —softly playing in the few minutes leading up to the start of class, to set the tone for students as they enter the room and find their seats. This creates a natural segue to the first section of the lesson, a brief introduction to the music of the troubadours. Using the high-resolution digital scans of the original manuscript for "A chantar" available on Gallica from the Bibliothèque nationale de France (n.d.), we then listened to the audio again while following the melodic contour on the projected manuscript. From there, we engage in a brief discussion about the characteristics of the notation in comparison to the neumes of plainchant, the range of interpretative decisions offered and demanded of performers, and—as a transitory move toward Haines's (2014) minstrel—the interplay of oral/written traditions in early notation. I dedicate approximately the first third of the class to the troubadours.

The topic of oral/written traditions can be effectively used to move from the somewhat-preserved troubadour music to the unknown music of the medieval minstrel, and finally, to the imaginative modern representations of the medieval minstrel. After a brief compare/contrast of the medieval minstrel and troubadour traditions, including social status/function and surviving musical examples, I use the minstrel to introduce the idea of musical medievalism, demonstrating a few musical signifiers at the piano, such as parallel fifths, use of Dorian mode and modal progressions, and double leading-tone cadences. Students are then asked to summarize and provide characteristics of the minstrel archetype as outlined by Haines (2014) and to suggest any other attendant features of the trope that they might add. These might include narrative elements like the convention of the minstrel-narrator/plot commentator or placement in narratively significant moments, or musical characteristics like the use of plucked string instruments, the influence of nineteenth-century interpretations of troubadour song, simple songs in style naïf, straightforward diatonic keys, or the frequent use of triple time. The use of Elizabethan-era sounds or Irish music, as one of Haines's more subtly touched-upon observations, will likely be worth guiding students to, as these are especially connected to the *Dragon Age* listening examples included in the lesson plan. This can also be a good time in the class session to incorporate a few of the student-provided examples of medieval minstrel scenes in film and television if you request that they contribute them via your online learning management system in advance of the class—additionally, I recommend sprinkling student examples throughout the class session as relevant.

After the group has established a useful summary of the medieval minstrel trope in cinema as outlined by Haines (2014), I begin to introduce examples from popular video games, starting with a video of a bard in *Skyrim* performing the ballad of Ragnar the Red. *Skyrim* is a medieval fantasy role-playing game originally released in 2011, selling over 30 million copies and accruing dozens of "Game of the Year" awards from gaming media organizations. In the game, the player character traverses an open world of snowy mountains, castles, villages, and dungeons on a quest to stop dragons from destroying the world—standard enough medievalist fare all around. Along the way, the player can see and hear bards in the game world's various taverns, such as the virtual performer Mikael, featured in the video example. After watching the video, students are asked to draw connections with Haines's archetype, whether in terms of musical characteristics or otherwise—from the simple style of the song to the rough primitivism of the digital performer's instrument. Keeping in mind that *Skyrim* is one of the most popular video games of the last decade and that this song enjoyed brief status as a meme, students might also volunteer their own knowledge about this song, or their experiences with *Skyrim*'s in-game bards. Here, it may be necessary to take care that the class not veer too sharply into the group sharing of marginally-relevant gaming anecdotes— but, in my experience, students were eager and focused in their engagement with the analysis of the video and the use of the minstrel trope in *Skyrim* broadly. Much productive discussion can be had through the visually rich exercise of comparing *Skyrim's* lute with early depictions of medieval and early modern instruments like the lute and gittern, as well as the nineteenth-century lyre guitars which *Skyrim's* "lute" more closely resembles. Topics of discussion ranged from analysis of the musical characteristics of the song to organological assessment of the virtual instrument, to the role of bards in retelling major political events and legends in *Skyrim's* world, all of which invited fruitful comparison with the imagined and real minstrels of the Haines and *Grove Music Online* readings, respectively. If your students take particular interest in the organology—the construction and appearance—of the instruments, or if you wish to guide their learning toward the historical medieval instruments, it can be useful to have videos or screenshots of less fantastical video game lutes for historical comparison as well. Depictions of instruments that more closely resemble early historical lutes and lute iconography can be found in *The Witcher 3*, *Ghost of A Tale*, *Mordhau*, and many other games. These closer examples afford an opportunity to comparatively discuss the features of historic lutes in relation to the video game depictions, building and reinforcing student understandings of the history of the lute—an instrument whose historic music will come more fully into the class's focus in the coming weeks when the course attends to sixteenth-century music. Or, if your students take more interest in the lyrical content of the songs, it can be productive to include the two *Skyrim* bard songs "The Age of Aggression" and "The Age of Oppression," whose player-influenceable texts retell or call for major political changes in the context of the game's world, inviting comparison with historic examples.

After this introductory video and discussion, I turn to a set of listening examples from *Dragon Age: Origins* in order to explore one strategy that the creators of popular representations of medieval minstrels sometimes use to enact their construction—the use of existing music associated with an early Modern or nostalgic past, in this case through the use of both Elizabethan ballad tunes and Irish folk songs. *Dragon Age: Inquisition* features a player character who traverses a land of forests, snowscapes, and castles on a quest to save the world by closing a portal leaking demons into the world of mortals; at the time of its release, it was developer Bioware's best-selling launch ever. After briefly introducing students to the minstrel character in the context of this game—a virtual bard named Maryden Halewell found, like *Skyrim's* bards, in the troped location of a tavern—I move on to the listening examples. The first of the two compare the video game's "Oh Grey Warden" with its late sixteenth-century source, "Packington's Pound." The second example sets the game's "Once We Were" in relief with the traditional Irish tune "South Wind," from which it derives its musical material; if students take particular interest in the use of Irish/Celtic-inspired music in fantasy medievalism, the instructor might also present Howard Shore's "Concerning Hobbits" from Peter Jackson's *Lord of the Rings* films, and direct students to Simon Nugent's (2020) "Celtic Music and Hollywood Cinema: Representation, Stereotype, and Affect." These examples can serve as a starting point for discussion of musical characteristics, how they relate to Haines's (2014) minstrel archetype, how we imagine and represent medieval music, and more. They also give the students the chance to reflect upon, analyze, and discuss the specific musical and sonic components of medievalism and representations of minstrel songs, in contrast with the visual emphasis in the earlier *Skyrim* example. Additionally, in the larger context of my course, the introduction of "Packington's Pound" serves as a useful foreshadowing of an upcoming class session on broadside ballads and other music of Elizabethan England; depending on time constraints, it can be useful to demonstrate other historic settings of this ballad tune to stimulate comparison and discussion about its transmission throughout the centuries.

For the final short section of the class session, I introduce a homework assignment and then "open the floor" to students' questions, comments, and other examples. The homework assignment takes the form of a brief online writing exercise with two parts of a length of approximately 250 words total with at least 75 words given to each part; this format follows a recurring 'journal' assigned for each era covered in the course and offers students a degree of flexibility in allocating their focus. The first component asks students to compare historic troubadour music with medieval sacred music (covered in the previous class session) in terms of the notation, instrumentation, degree of preservation, social function, etc. The second component asks them to find an example of Haines's (2014) minstrel archetype in media of their choosing (or to revisit the example they chose for class), write a brief description of how their chosen example fits or contrasts with Haines's criteria, and reflect on their own associations with—or other thoughts on—the minstrel trope and musical medievalism more broadly. While I supplied a list of examples for students to use if they couldn't think of any, I encouraged them to find their own examples not on the list, which most students did. Finally, in the days following the class session, I wrote and posted a response to some of the themes and topics that had emerged during the class session and student discussion on the class's online course page; for example, since many students had found the poor synchronization of the animation and the music in *Skyrim* comical, I took the opportunity to share with them a video by the classical music comedy duo Two Set Violin which lampoons similarly poor synchronization and unrealistic musical performances in popular films. In this way, the lesson on medievalism facilitated connections to broader questions of musical representation and afforded the opportunity to introduce students to popular comedic and educational content.

Student Response and Project Outcomes

The student response to this topic and class session was generally positive. I found that students engaged with the material and class discussion far more, and with greater interest, than what I had encountered in my earlier experience teaching a medieval music lesson without significant incorporation of the contemporary examples and 'medievalism' angle. For some students, this was the first time they had been in a course that used video games as objects of serious attention, or their first time engaging in academic media analysis with a product of popular culture in general. Even so, the students offered numerous relevant examples, often from unexpected domains such as musicals and card games. Further, their rich engagement in discussion raised many thought-provoking points and questions about medieval music, popular cultural representation of the past, and the relationship between cultural imagination and memory, while drawing on student disciplinary insights from fields such as media studies, history, and music. In addition to enriching the entire group's understanding of these topics, these disciplinary insights offered students the valuable opportunity to practice communicating their field's perspectives to a general audience--an invaluable skill in our interdisciplinary world. Perhaps due to my own musical background, I believe this was especially valuable for the musically trained students communicating technical musical concepts, given the unique challenges and importance of developing this skill for musicians.

However, there are a few caveats which deserve mentioning. It is perhaps obvious, but not all students will be equally interested or engaged in a conversation about medieval fantasy and video games. While this genre and medium are widely popular, some students reported that they were not gamers or fans of medieval fantasy; while they were still familiar with the trope and capable of effectively engaging with the material, their relation to the content did not optimally reflect the cultural immediacy I had intended with this lesson. As most students provided examples from film or television series, it is likely that a more balanced focus on these media sources, in addition to video games, would have more effectively engaged a broader range of students. On the one hand, it is appropriate for a college course to introduce you to new topics and ideas that you have not previously encountered. On the other hand, insofar as the class was designed with the intention of making students feel that their own popular culture and interests are represented and worth scholarly analysis, then it should be noted that a class on fantasy medievalism in video games will offer different degrees and kinds of engagement for different students—not only in the domain of 'video games' specifically, but students who are not greatly interested in pop culture medievalism in general. To that end, this class session ought to be employed as just one part of a balanced, diverse curriculum and course design that attends to other perspectives, traditions, and interests throughout the overall course. Conversely, fan enthusiasm for the topic may require the instructor to maintain the appropriate line of relevant academic discourse in this class session's discussion sessions; in so doing, however, care should be taken to redirect their enthusiasm without stifling it.

A third possible caveat to consider, depending on your learning goals for the course, is that this lesson plan necessarily reduced the amount of time I was able to spend on the historical medieval secular song of the troubadours, as well as other historical medieval music. For the purposes of my course, this was not necessarily a problem as my goal was not to only educate students in historical genres but also to facilitate their reflection on the manifestations and refractions of these cases in their own lived experiences, but it merits considering for adoption in other contexts, such as courses with a more strictly historical focus. Nonetheless, this general approach of blending historical perspective with present-day medievalism can be fruitfully adapted into a variety of course settings such as history, media studies, critical theory, art history, or gender studies to provide for engaging comparative cases in media representation; for example, depictions of medieval society and city development in video games like *Anno 1404*, medieval manuscript inspired art styles in the games *Pentiment* and *Inkulinati*, or representations of medieval politics, fantasy orientalism, or gender roles in the television series *Game of Thrones*. Alternatively, an entire music course (or course unit) might be designed around the study of musical medievalism and the moving image more broadly, with lessons based around each of Haines's (2014) archetypal signifiers (chant, trumpet fanfares, church bells, etc.).

Thinking beyond the medieval period or music, there is a practically endless number of video games instructors might draw upon when teaching topics on a wide range of historical eras; James Cook (2021) has explored the broad and varied ways that video games have played with history for decades. Other video game genres far removed from medievalism have much to explore regarding the embedded aesthetic, cultural, and ideological assumptions of the societies that produce and consume them. A course on Orientalism would be well-suited to analyzing the visual and musical language of archetypal "desert level" found in many classic platformers, with several entries in the *Super Mario* series likely providing the most well-known examples. A course in film or media studies, history of science fiction, or music might fruitfully invert the medievalist orientation offered in this chapter, instead turning its pedagogical gaze from the imagined past of medievalism to the imagined future of cyberpunk, examining the transfer of representational tropes from films such as *Blade Runner* (1982) into video games like *Deus Ex* (2000) and *Cyberpunk 2077* (2020).

Conclusion

My experience incorporating video game examples into the curriculum of an undergraduate music appreciation class and, with it, bringing the study of musical medievalism into the teaching of the music of the medieval period, suggests that this approach can be a significant driver of student engagement and learning. These popular works can serve as an accessible entry point for historical education through comparison with the past. In addition to facilitating historical connections and comparisons, this approach encourages students to reflect upon the tropes and archetypes they encounter in popular culture today and to think critically about the roles and uses of music, history, and imagery in the representational languages and traditions of that culture. The range of musical examples—from historical troubadour songs to sixteenth-century English ballads and Irish folk tunes to newly-composed material—engages students with questions about history and the past, as well as how we represent, reimagine, rework, and reinvent history and the past in the present. Further, since students are encouraged to bring in, discuss, and write about examples they have seen, the material of the class can be co-constructed with the students, centering their interests and offering a greater immediacy and relevancy in relation to their own experiences. It encourages students to think about how music operates in and across media, and how video games carry forward the significative codes of cinema and other popular traditions. Although this lesson plan was specifically oriented around music, the general model can be adapted with content relevant to a variety of fields; it could also be implemented with a deeper level of technical musical analysis in a course designed for music majors, opening the possibility of composition exercises and other forms of student engagement. While not all students take equal interest in video games or medieval fantasy, these topical areas can nonetheless serve as effective components of a diverse curriculum that holistically incorporates a variety of relevant student interests.

References

Bailey, N. M. (2012). The importance of a New Literacies stance in teaching English Language Arts. In S.M. Miller & M.B. McVee (Eds.), *Multimodal Composing in Classrooms: Learning and Teaching for the Digital World* (pp. 44-62). Routledge.

Barton, G. (2018). *Music learning and teaching in culturally and socially diverse contexts: Implications for classroom practice.* Palgrave Macmillan.

Bibliothèque nationale de France, Département des manuscrits. (n.d.) Manuscrit du Roi, Français 844. Facsimile URL: https://gallica.bnf.fr/ark:/12148/btv1b8 4192440/f423.item#

Butt, J. (2002). *Playing with history: The historical approach to musical performance.* Cambridge University Press.

Cook, J. (2020). Sonic medievalism, world building, and cultural identity in fantasy video games. In K. Fugelso (Ed.), *Studies in Medievalism XXIX: Politics and Medievalism* (Vol. 29). Boydell and Brewer.

Cook, J. (2021). Game music and history. In M. Fritsch & T. Summers (Eds.), *The Cambridge Companion to Video Game Music* (pp.343–58). Cambridge University Press.

Cook, K. (2018). Beyond (the) Halo: Chant in video games. *Studies in Medievalism XXVII: Authenticity, Medievalism, Music* (Vol. 29). Boydell and Brewer.

Fink, L. D. (2013). *Creating significant learning experiences: An integrated approach to designing college courses.* Wiley.

Gushee, L., Rastall, R., & Klausner, D. (2013). Minstrel. In *Grove Music Online.* https://doi-org.turing.library.northwestern.edu/10.1093/gmo/9781561592630.article.18748

Haefeli, S. (2022). *Teaching music history with cases: A teacher's guide.* Routledge.

Haines, J. (2014). *Music in films on the Middle Ages: Authenticity Vs. fantasy.* Routledge.

Kamien, R. (2022). *Music: An appreciation.* McGraw Hill.

Prensky, M. (2001). Digital natives, Digital immigrants. *On the Horizon 9(5)*, 1-6.

Nugent, S. (2020). Celtic music and Hollywood cinema: Representation, stereotype, and affect. In J. Cook, Alexander K., & A. Whittaker (Eds.), *Recomposing the Past: Representations of Early Music on the Stage and Screen* (pp. 107-123). Routledge.

Stevens, J., Butterfield, A., and Karp. T. (2001). Troubadours, trouvères. In *Grove Music Online.* https://doi-org.turing.library.northwestern.edu/10.1093/gmo/9781561592630.article.28468

Walker, R. (2001). The rise and fall of philosophies of music education: Looking backwards in order to see ahead. *Research Studies in Music Education, 17(1)*, 3–18.

Zancanella, D., Hall, L. & Pence, P. (2000). Computer games as literature. In A. Goodwyn (Ed.), *English in the Digital Age: Information and Communications Technology (ITC) and the Teaching of English* (pp. 87-102). Bloomsbury Academic.

Chapter 9

Level Up your Classroom Management with Classcraft Gamification

Leeda Copley

University of Central Oklahoma

Abstract: Copley discusses the use of clear gamification goals to motivate students to learn more deeply, noting also that poor gamification strategies stress students out and can lead to negative learning goals. She gives the example of using Classcraft.com, a free resource, to help increase students' learning and retention of information.

Keywords: gamification; sociology; Classcraft

***

Introduction

As an educator in sociology, I can't get this statistic out of my mind: the U.S. Bureau of Labor Statistics put out a report in 2021 that showed Baby Boomers changed jobs a dozen times in their lifetime. Now, half of those job changes happened when they were quite young—from ages 18 to 24—but the other half happened well into adulthood (US Bureau of Labor Statistics, 2021). Knowing that students will change jobs at least a few times within their lifetime, I want to prepare my students for their first job after college as well as subsequent job changes, and I fight with myself about how best to do this. I personally want to create what Paul Hanstedt (2018) refers to as "wicked students," empowering students to be nimble, creative problem solvers who can work autonomously and adapt to a changing world.

There has been significant talk about the importance of building "soft skills" in our students (Forbes Coaches Council, 2019; Rockwood, 2021), but even then there is debate about which skills we should be focusing on. Resiliency? Creativity? Problem-solving? Basic communication? Emotional intelligence? Curiosity? Relationship skills? I do not claim to have an answer, but I do have a suggestion for how we can flip our educational scripts to make room for all of these and more: gamify our classes.

Arguably, the most important shift in a gamified class—as compared to traditional classes—is a focus on student choice, with multiple pathways for a student to pass the class. Implicit in this is the opportunity for them to keep trying until they pass. This encourages students to adopt a growth mindset; if one technique does not work for them, there are others to try, and no shame in trying again. In much the same way that Mario cannot move on to the next level until he defeats the boss, the students often must try and try again before they can move onto the next unit or topic. The goal is as much about "failing better next time" as it is about "winning," which is the apex of the growth mindset (Dweck, 2007).

The language of gaming is truly ubiquitous for anyone born after about 1970, regardless of whether they identify as a gamer or not. One study found that the average age of gamers was 37 years old (Erenli, 2013), so this is not just about the very young. Concepts like "XP or experience points," "boss battles," and "leveling up" are understood almost universally among college students of all ages, regardless of whether they play video games or not. Gamification is a way to leverage the fact that our college students are mostly "digital natives" (Kiryakova et al., 2014; Medica Ružić & Dumančić, 2015; Prensky, 2001), with 97% of youths playing video games and over three-quarters of American households owning video games (Erenli, 2013).

Gamification in the Literature – What Do We Know? What Do We Not Know?

Gamification burst onto the educational scene soon after Deterding and his colleagues (2011) gave their presentation on how game design elements could be taken out of software and put into other fields to make things more "playful" (Martí-Parreño et al., 2016; Miller, 2013; Swacha, 2021). In the dozen years since then, gamifying classes has become a controversial trend, because much of it is still unproven by empirical studies. If we're being perfectly honest with ourselves, much of it is still untested and assumed because we have not come to any sort of clear consensus of what constitutes gamification in educational settings, and we certainly have not empirically evaluated it in rigorous, valid, and reliable ways. Thanks to a documented publication bias in the gamification literature (Dicheva & Dichev, 2015; Rabah et al., 2018), we should be wary that the literature that exists may be overstating positive outcomes. The literature is still hedging on "could" statements, about gamification having "potential" or being "promising" (Caponetto et al., 2014; Majuri et al., 2018; Manzano-León et al., 2021; Martí-Parreño et al., 2016; Oliveira et al., 2023).

It is notable and encouraging that what gamification research is out there is not specific to any one field or discipline; research shows that it can work for fields as different as science, language, health, software engineering, and arts (Caponetto et al., 2014; Dicheva et al., 2015).

Self Determination Theory

Despite the inconclusiveness of much of the research into gamification, we do see a few important and useful ideas. When done well, gamification taps into our psychological needs for autonomy, feeling competent, and relatedness to others—the entire gist of Deci's Self-Determination Theory (Surendeleg et al., 2014; Van Roy & Zaman, 2018).

As educators, we need to understand that our students want to feel like they have control over their experience of the game and provide them with real and meaningful choices to make. An important component of this is providing multiple pathways to their goals, such as giving points for writing assignments or class discussions. More introverted students will appreciate being able to choose the writing assignment, while outgoing students will happily speak up in front of the class. The key thing is that students can choose their path based on their personal strengths.

Valuing students' choices leads them to feel more competent with the academic material in the class and should help them learn in ways that they deem best for them. Of course, feelings of competence (i.e., confidence) and actual competence in the academic discipline are different matters, and we need to build our courses and games in such a way that preserves honest, summative assessment. No one is arguing that the gamified classroom should only be about participation efforts and not discipline knowledge, in the same way, that no one is seriously arguing that traditional classes should grade entirely on participation and not knowledge acquisition or discipline skills.

Teamwork is the key to providing students with an interpersonal connection, and that sense of relatedness to both their peers and the class at large. Collaboration and working in groups are also key to building students' soft skills, especially interpersonal problem-solving and relationship skills. To this end, instructors should consider giving awards or positive recognition for several different types of successes—not just the obvious academic ones (Mitchell et al., 2013). This also ties well into social and emotional learning, which has been tied to many positive outcomes for students (Durlak et al., 2011).

Why the Lack of High-Quality Research on Gamification Does Not Bother Me

Perhaps the most compelling argument for why we should gamify our classes despite the lack of empirical evidence and consensus is simple: gamification largely makes use of our already-recognized best practices in pedagogy (Stott & Neustaedter, 2013). Detractors may call gamification "superficial" or "manipulation," but underneath the bells and whistles of the game is real pedagogy.

In Lee Sheldon's (2020) now classic *The Multiplayer Classroom: Designing Coursework as a Game*, the students are still writing papers even if they call it "crafting," taking tests despite calling it "fighting monsters," and doing class presentations even if they call it "completing quests." Gamifying your class does not mean throwing away everything that has been shown repeatedly to work in the classroom—it is merely reframing the discussion about it to get students more motivated to do the work. By the way, Sheldon only changed the way he talked about pedagogy, which is sometimes seen as gamification-lite, not true gamification. However, even this simple shift in the language around grading, from punishing mistakes to celebrating successes, led to his average grades bumping up a full letter grade (Sheldon, 2020).

College education grand doyen Ken Bain has made a career out of convincing his fellow professors that the difference between good instructors and everyone else is that the best educators challenge and inspire their students into a growth mindset. By challenging students and then giving them the autonomy to discover their own way, we help students find their own passion—and develop compassion along the way (Bain, 2004). He took it further in *Super Courses* to argue that educators need to build a "natural critical learning environment" that values students' autonomy and encourages them to work with others to answer the "big, beautiful questions" in life (Bain, 2021). While neither of his books deals with gamification directly, it should not be difficult to see how gamification can check several of these boxes. A good, gamified course should challenge students while giving them the autonomy to creatively problem-solve their way to a desired grade.

Likewise, when gamified well, courses should push students to think and act more creatively, since instructors should give more leeway in the modes of demonstrating their learning; anecdotally, my students can turn in traditional essays or more creative photo essays, write songs or create artwork for some assignments. Student autonomy is key to encouraging self-directed learners with their own intrinsic motivation to answer the big questions in their own lives (Bain, 2021). Gamifying our classes allows our students the freedom to make mistakes and try again, which is arguably some of the best training for life in our complex world, regardless of our academic discipline (Hanstedt, 2018).

Finally, I suspect that Bain would support the use of teamwork in gamified classes since peer-to-peer mentoring and relationships are so key in his conceptualizations of developing students' inherent passions for learning. Engaging students in ingenious ways, respecting their abilities, and setting high standards are all important to getting the sage off of the stage, so to speak (Bain, 2004, 2021). In gamified classes, the faculty isn't the focus—we are truly the guide on the side, pointing to a goal and letting students find their own paths to get there. Cultivating that culture of peer support should encourage students to feel more connected, share their knowledge, and support their peers in ways that should help with student retention (Mitchell et al., 2013). For instructors interested in collaborative teaching partnerships with their students or democratic teaching methods (Brookfield & Preskill, 2012; Cook-Sather et al., 2014), gamified classes provide ample opportunities for faculty to share the power and risks in the learning process. By trusting students and clearly communicating with them, students can take far more control over the daily class activities.

Four (or So) Ingredients for Successful Gamification

There have been multiple attempts to pin down and extract what exactly works in gamification. Stott and Neustaedter (2013) have proposed a conceptual framework that is useful for this discussion, as it focuses on four dynamics that have been consistently demonstrated in the literature to work in gamified courses: the "freedom to fail," quick feedback, progression or scaffolded instruction, and storytelling.

Giving students the "freedom to fail" repeatedly teaches them resiliency and creative problem-solving, empowers them to make progress, and helps them feel like "an active protagonist in their learning" (Manzano-León et al., 2021). Students can try and try again, with relatively low stakes for each attempt, which allows students to make mistakes and experiment with different ways to solve a problem. This is not necessarily about giving students unlimited re-do's on a summative test, it is more about giving lots of low-stakes formative assessments to build up to any summative assessment (Dicheva et al., 2015; Kiryakova et al., 2014; Stott & Neustaedter, 2013; Turan et al., 2016). When students get comfortable with failure, those uncertain aspects of the game (e.g., random events) become part of the fun (Erenli, 2013; Miller, 2013).

Closely related to the freedom to fail is the necessity of rapid feedback. It is not sufficient just to give a lot of low-stakes assessments and assignments to your students, you also must provide them with quick (ideally instant) feedback (Miller, 2013; Stott & Neustaedter, 2013). This is what provides students with that gaming logic of trying repeatedly until they make it to the next level. We do need to keep in mind the importance of smaller, immediate goals—as well as keeping tasks specific, clear, and concrete so the feedback cycle stays short (Dicheva et al., 2015). Put another way, cut a larger quest or assignment into smaller tasks so students get regular, immediate feedback on their progress. This strategy has the added benefit of instructors catching student mistakes earlier, which can minimize students' frustrations and feelings that their mistakes wasted time.

It is not sufficient to just throw a lot of low-stakes assignments at your students, there must be a clear progression that is visible to students. Accrual grading through experience points plus visible progress through levels or progress bars is one of the best-documented aspects of gamification (Dicheva et al., 2015; Majuri et al., 2018; Nah et al., 2014; Stott & Neustaedter, 2013). The progression dynamic comes straight out of Beth Kemp Benson's (1997) idea of scaffolded instruction (Stott & Neustaedter, 2013). In short, Benson argues for pedagogy that guides students through information in categories to help focus their attention. If a student is struggling, does not know where to start, or has to restart after making a mistake, scaffolded learning can help (Benson, 1997; Stott & Neustaedter, 2013). There is a clear progression to the game, so students should know where to start if their quests are set up in such a way as to be linear (e.g., students must complete step one before moving on to step two). Students at lower levels must "unlock" later material by demonstrating proficiency in the earlier material first (Dicheva et al., 2015). Even in classes where the material is not set up linearly, like in my own sociology classes, providing the linear progression of levels helps students know where they are in the course. If they know they should be at level ten at this point in the semester, and they are only on level seven, they know they need to pick up the pace and do more assignments. Note that making this concrete progression visible to students at all times becomes a sort of rapid feedback in and of itself (Stott & Neustaedter, 2013).

The final ingredient for a successfully gamified class is storytelling (Deterding et al., 2011; Dicheva et al., 2015; Erenli, 2013; Nah et al., 2014; Sheldon, 2020; Stott & Neustaedter, 2013). The idea that the game is external to the real world, and on some level fantastic, has been shown to increase students' interest in the topics and motivation to do work and may have the ability to positively affect retention (Dicheva et al., 2015; Nah et al., 2013, 2014; Stott & Neustaedter, 2013). There have been arguments in many corners of education that stories can help provide students with context and be extremely effective in increasing student engagement (Bain, 2004; Stott & Neustaedter, 2013).

There are a few other concepts or dynamics worth mentioning in the literature, even if they do not have as much robust evidence supporting them. The ability for students to customize their experience, be it by choosing an avatar or choosing the difficulty of their pathway, has some interesting early results that show increased student motivation (Dicheva et al., 2015; Freitas et al., 2017; Oliveira et al., 2023). Student competition and cooperation have mixed results, suggesting that a little competition is good but too much can be counterproductive (Manzano-León et al., 2021; Mitchell et al., 2013; Stott & Neustaedter, 2013; Toda et al., 2018; Turan et al., 2016). Finally, conceptualizing gamified courses as both "governed by clear rules" yet unpredictable with uncertain outcomes (e.g., random events or random picking of a student to answer a question) is an important balance to strike to keep students interested but not feeling like the game is unfair (Erenli, 2013). The expectedness of clear rules is countered by the erraticism of the game's random mechanics to keep students from becoming too comfortable.

The Downside

We do need to make sure that gamification is not just superficial "edutainment." Those who are against gamification make some fair points that, when done poorly, gamifying the classroom is just adding more stress and competition to our students' already-strained bandwidth (Rabah et al., 2018; Toda et al., 2018). Is it an "aimless distraction" that disrupts true learning if students are more focused on getting their avatar a new suit than the course material? Of course, it is. We need to design our games to tap into learners' intrinsic motivations, not their extrinsic motivations for badges (Sandusky, 2015). Done well, we want our students to still be interacting more with their course material, and getting a grade that reflects their academic abilities, not their gaming abilities to grind through menial tasks for XP. Even when done well, there are some qualitative findings that gamification can cause jealousy among students (Turan et al., 2016), and leaderboards are not recommended because they can be strongly associated with negative effects on students (Furdu et al., 2017; Toda et al., 2018). The competition fostered by leaderboards is especially mixed, with some research showing it can motivate (Fotaris et al., 2016; Huang & Hew, 2015; Ortiz-Rojas et al., 2019), but others showing it tends to demotivate students (Devers & Gurung, 2015; Nicholson, 2013). The reality is likely that competition connects with some students but not all, depending on the extroversion or introversion of the individual students (Codish & Ravid, 2014), and whether the student is new to the material or has prior knowledge (Abramovich et al., 2013).

If we recognize that the detractors have described exactly what gamification should not be, then we can work to make certain that our use of gamification does not do this. For example, one study found that students were demotivated by leaderboards and penalties, and those who did not understand the rules of the game fared poorly (Toda et al., 2018). This urges us to keep the rules simple and make certain that all students understand them. Not surprisingly, the same study found that if there are problems with the gaming system not working as expected, students become very frustrated (Toda et al., 2018).

When presenting experimental results that show sixth graders who learned by gamification had higher cognitive load levels than those in the non-gamified control group, Turan and their colleagues (2016) had to quickly qualify their findings. We do not know if that higher cognitive load was because the students were actually learning more, or if they just had to think more because they had the addition of the game itself (i.e., they had to think about their studies and the game). Worse yet, they could not determine if the cognitive load levels had been hijacked by the game, meaning students were thinking more, but only about the game and not the material. They concluded that this was unlikely, given that the gamified students achieved more and scored higher (Turan et al., 2016) but this provides a useful warning to instructors. We need to remember that our students have limited bandwidth, and ideally should keep our game dynamics simple so they can focus on the discipline knowledge and not the game itself.

As for arguments that gamification is manipulation, and therefore somehow disrespectful of students (Dicheva et al., 2015; Rabah et al., 2018; Toda et al., 2018), all of us can benefit from considering the implications of this regardless of whether we gamify our classes or not. Personally, I am happy to manipulate or persuade my students into doing their work, and the feedback I have received from students does not suggest that they feel manipulated. If anything, they feel valued and respected because their faculty is taking the time and effort to make the learning process more fun. However, the concerns about intrinsic and extrinsic motivations are valid. We want our students to be driven by a desire to know, a desire to accomplish, and a desire for stimulating experiences—not by "shoulds," to avoid guilt, or to satisfy the teacher (Buckley & Doyle, 2016; Sandusky, 2015). Keeping these motivation types in mind can help us create more effective game components, assignments, and activities.

An Assumption that "Fun" Is Good

Basically all of the literature on gamification has the underlying assumption that making education fun is a positive thing (Arnold, 2014; Deterding et al., 2011; Erenli, 2013; Kim, 2015; Majuri et al., 2018; Manzano-León et al., 2021; Martí-Parreño et al., 2016; Medica Ružić & Dumančić, 2015; Miller, 2013; Nah et al., 2013; Surendeleg et al., 2014). Indeed, much of this literature talks at length about how gamification supports active learning by increasing students' motivation and engagement with the class (Buckley & Doyle, 2016; Hallifax et al., 2019; Kiryakova et al., 2014; Manzano-León et al., 2021; Martí-Parreño et al., 2016; Miller, 2013; Oliveira et al., 2023; Sandusky, 2015). However, I would be negligent as a sociologist if I failed to play devil's advocate here and ask if making education fun is an inherently good thing.

Sociologists like to talk about the Disneyfication (or Disneyization) of society, whereby mundane activities are turned into magical experiences, generally so a corporation can charge us more money for them (Bryman, 2004). A classic example of this is a well-known company that sells stuffed animals at much higher-than-market prices because the shopping experience is turned into a magical fantasy of the customer choosing and building their new "friend." It does not help that the homogenization that makes it easier to consume is associated with dumbing down and sanitizing our places and experiences (Bryman, 2004). At a time when universities and colleges seem bent on consumeristic business models, judging their faculty by credit-hour production, the widescale Disneyfication of our classes would be a nightmare for higher education. The concern that faculty could be replaced by gamified MOOCs is real, and should not be taken lightly (Ofosu-Ampong, 2020).

All of this leads us to the problem in education of grappling with how much fun we should make our classes. If students come to expect that all educational pursuits should be fun and that they are entitled to only do activities that interest them, we are failing to nurture their emotional growth as human beings. Not everything in their future lives or careers will interest them or pique their curiosity, and we do owe it to them to give them practice doing hard work that does not interest them. Students need to learn internal self-direction so they will be able to get through hard activities in their futures. I will be the first to admit I do not have the answer to these questions, and I have not seen any research that answers them for us. While I highly encourage my fellow faculty members to consider gamifying parts or all their classes, I would absolutely fight against any forced, top-down efforts to make education more palatable to students by gamifying across an entire college or university. Efforts to turn gamification into a market advantage by a university should be fought at all costs as an affront to academic freedom. I personally turned to Classcraft as an all-in-one option for gamification because I wanted to gamify my classes, not because I was forced to use the system. This is an important distinction—educators know their students best and should be allowed to choose if gamification makes sense for them and to choose the system that meets their needs.

After researching several systems, I ultimately chose Classcraft for two major reasons. First, Classcraft does a lot of the work in setting up "the game," instead of more manual systems where I would have needed to design badges or write scripts. Secondly, it was free. The system is completely free to students and has a freemium-style structure for instructors, which makes it ideal for both. The instructor-paid, premium version includes more customization options for your students and more tools, which is great but far from necessary for most instructors. The case study that I will provide below hopes to promote gamification more broadly, even as I focus on Classcraft; you can accomplish much of what Classcraft does using other systems or manually without a system.

The Classcraft Platform

Classcraft.com is a free website that provides the structure of a game to overlay your regular course. Classcraft is a Certified B Corporation, meaning it functions more like a nonprofit despite being a corporation and developed in part thanks to a $400,000 grant from the Government of Canada (Canada Economic Development, 2018). Houghton Mifflin Harcourt, or HMH, acquired Classcraft in May 2023, and it has not yet been made clear if or how this will change the system after the 2023-2024 school year finishes (Young, 2023). Even though the Classcraft system is set up for K-12, there is a burgeoning group of higher education faculty who use it regularly.

The system works like a live grade, with students knowing exactly what level they are on at all times. All the action is in the real world—students must do the real work of the class to see their avatar level up; there are no students grinding through the game on their devices during class. Faculty set how many Experience Points (XP) are necessary for each level up, what level students need to reach in the game and the different ways to receive XP. Instructors also generally put students into teams for the duration of the semester, though students can of course help create and name those teams.

Students earn Experience points (XP) by completing work and these can never be taken away. Instructors determine before the class begins what the different "positive behaviors" are that will merit awarding XP, but faculty always can manually add more if a student does something worthy. Classcraft makes suggestions, but it is up to the instructor to choose how much XP will be awarded for each good deed.

Hearts are a measure of health and can be taken away if a student breaks a rule or misses a question, for example. The instructor also sets out these "negative behaviors" and how many hearts will be taken away for each before the semester begins. If a student's health falls to zero, the euphemism for character death is "falling" or "falling in battle." If a student's health falls to zero, their whole team takes a hit to their health, and the fallen student must do extra work in the form of a pledge. The system will randomly select from a handful of pledges that the instructor set up before the semester began, and the fallen student must complete that extra assignment before they can continue on in the class. Their character is frozen and cannot get more XP until the pledge is completed.

Crystals are consumed when a student uses a power. As students level up, they gain different "powers" which the faculty can set up to support the goals of the class; the suggestion is that some of the powers should help in the "game," but others should help the student in the class (e.g., can ask the instructor one question during the next test). Hearts and Crystals both regenerate a little bit each day, with the instructor able to set the regeneration rate.

Gold is like extra credit given for extra effort and used to buy avatar clothing or pets. Again, there is no real money involved for students, so this is truly extra. Gold is part of the premium, paid instructor experience, but is far from necessary. For instructors who do pay the premium, the system is set up to give a little bit of gold for most positive behaviors (as well as XP), but this can be changed by the instructor before the semester begins.

Students get to choose what character class they want to be, and the appearance of their avatars, avatars' clothes, and avatar's backgrounds. Classcraft recently expanded its avatars to make certain there are gender-neutral choices for each of the classes. The four classes are Mages (have the most Crystals for using powers), Guardians (have the most Hearts to avoid "falling"), Healers (balanced), and Adventurers/Explorers for students with no interest in the game and no avatar. In my anecdotal experience with the game over several classes in several semesters, most students choose their character class based on the appearances of the avatars, not my descriptions of who has the most health or crystals.

While there is no leaderboard—research shows they can be detrimental (Toda et al., 2018)—there is still social pressure to level up when the levels are publicly shown to the entire class. This means you should not make Classcraft the entire grade for your students, as this could potentially lead to FERPA violations since students could technically see the grades of their fellow students. Instructors can limit whether logged-in students can see only the statistics of their own team or of the whole class, but many instructors pull up the class dashboard at the start of each class, meaning the students can see where they stand compared to others. (Many instructors, myself included, keep the class dashboard up in the background throughout the class period so points can be added quickly during class.)

The Class Tools

The suite of tools available in the Classcraft system is comprehensive and requires relatively little setup from the faculty member after the first time.

The Wheel of Destiny random picker can pick students or teams for a question or activity. This can keep educators from unconsciously favoring any one student or group of students for asking questions. While I do not like to cold-call individual students to answer in class, having the system pick an entire team to answer a question gives some sense of safety to anxious students and helps students work on their collaboration. It has been my experience in multiple classes that if a whole team is struggling with a question, students will often ask if they can help answer, even if they are not on the team. Your educational goals may differ, but I like seeing those high-level efforts at collaboration.

The "Riders of the Vay" is a random event generator to start each class with something fun, and the faculty provides the list of those random events at the beginning of the semester. Classcraft has several suggestions for random events for instructors to use or personalize, but these are not necessarily meant to be specific to the class material. Examples from the case study course I will discuss below included a random student winning 30 gold if they could answer a riddle, or 200XP going to the healer who could say hello in the most languages.

Formative review sessions are the dramatic "Boss Battles," which require the instructor to create the questions beforehand, but the new Elda Training Grounds allows for the drama without preset questions. I did not use these tools in the case study discussed below but have used Boss Battles in other classes. It can be a fun way to review for an upcoming exam since students have to answer enough questions to beat the boss. My students preferred to do battles without the music on, and in groups so they could collaborate on answers, but it can be a bit stressful losing health.

The "Shrine of the Ancients" kudos board encourages students to support each other. A student can leave a note praising an individual student, a team, or the class at large. I have seen students leave notes that say "thanks," "good job," or even "congratulations" to the whole class for surviving a test.

There are currently three premium-only tools. The "White Mountain" timer and "Forest Run" stopwatch functions can be useful in classes where students do bursts of writing or speaking, or if you teach long classes with breaks. I generally only used the timer for timing breaks but could see where it would work well as a test or activity timer. The "Treasures of Tavuros" Grade Converter is also a premium tool because it gives students XP and gold based on their performance on traditional assignments or tests. The instructor inputs all the students' real-world grades on, say, a midterm exam, and the students receive gold and XP for each percentage point they have over a passing grade. The instructor can personalize what the passing score is, and how much students get for every percentage point over passing, and can even set it to take hearts away for each point below passing.

Faculty have complete control over how the game is used and can pick and choose which tools would best support their students' needs. Some of the tools are clearly more useful for PreK-12, such as the "Makus Valley" volume meter. Classcraft also has a dedicated messaging board that may not be useful since so many university courses have a separate, required learning management system with dedicated messaging.

If you have assignments that need to be completed in a particular order, Classcraft Quests is a useful tool. A quest combines a fictional story with student activities and assessments. In other words, students must get a question right before they can read the next section of the story. Students can see their progress through the quest on maps provided by Classcraft. There is a Quests Marketplace where other teachers have uploaded quests (assessments and stories), but these are primarily from PreK-12 teachers and of limited use to faculty teaching college courses. However, it is relatively easy to set up a quest from scratch, and instructors keep their quests in My Library so they can be used in multiple classes. Classcraft has premade fictional journeys in their "Story Mode," which faculty then pair with their discipline material to create a quest. I have used this in other classes (not the case study class below) with assignments that have a more structured process. For example, you can set up a quest to help students through writing an academic essay with step one picking a topic, step two searching for journal articles, step three making an outline, and so forth. A useful feature of the Classcraft Quest system is that instructors can branch pathways so students who are struggling can be branched off to an extra section to get more information or practice. For example, the student who is struggling with their paper could get a branched pathway that includes the step, 'Take your paper to the writing center' or 'Come see me during office hours.'

Is This Only for Young Kids?

There is a small but committed community of higher education instructors using Classcraft, even though it was designed with K-12 students in mind. While much of the budding literature on gamification has focused on younger students, there is considerable research on gamification working in college courses (Caponetto et al., 2014; Dicheva et al., 2015; W. H.-Y. Huang & Soman, 2013; Mitchell et al., 2013; Sheldon, 2020; Surendeleg et al., 2014; Van Roy & Zaman, 2018).

In my experience, even older, adult learners and nontraditional students (those with significant lived experiences between high school and university) seem to appreciate the game dynamic. Traditional students are still very much playing video games in their leisure time, and anecdotally, I have not had any sense that students feel like they have "outgrown" games. Before first adopting the Classcraft platform, I mentally prepared myself thinking that most students were not going to be grown gamers like myself, and therefore not into the game. I figured that in that first class of 25 students, maybe a few would really get into the game and the rest would merely humor me. In fact, in that class and each successive class I've used Classcraft in since, the proportion is the exact opposite. A few are not into the game (and remain Explorers) and the rest take to it like it's second nature. Even those who are not gamers have grown up within gaming culture and understand its vocabulary and processes.

A Note About Adaptation

The literature agrees that gamification works best if there is adaptation and personalization (Oliveira et al., 2023), but there is no real consensus about what exactly that means. Of course, it makes sense to tailor your game to your students and how they are doing, but there isn't yet much research into ways that this can be done. One attempt to pin this problem down suggested that games should make use of "static adaptation," like character types that are chosen once at the beginning, and "dynamic adaptation" where changes occur throughout the class as students improve (Hallifax et al., 2019).

The Classcraft system currently uses static adaptation by providing students with a choice of player types. Students who worry about struggling in class likely want to be Guardians with lots of health, high achievers who are into the game are likely drawn towards becoming a Mage, so they have maximum crystals for powers. Students who are not at all interested in the game can remain Explorers (or Adventurers) the entire semester.

Dynamic adaptation, such as the game getting progressively harder as students improve, is not built into the Classcraft game, but there are ways that instructors can make things progressively more challenging for their students. You can change the Experience Points needed for a level-up while a class is running, but I would not suggest such a massive change to the basic rules of the game unless you've made it abundantly clear to the students that this change is going to happen at this particular time in the semester for everyone. (Also note that the change in the rules would affect all students, not just those who have earned the increased difficulty by excelling in the class.)

The kinder, more reasonable way to dynamically adapt your class as the semester progresses is to provide increasingly harder questions in The Wheel of Destiny (Random Picker), in Boss Battles (Formative Review), and in the new Elda Training Grounds (Quick Review). If you still have traditional tests or assignments in the Quests that get progressively more difficult, this would also count as dynamic adaptation. Making certain that students still have multiple pathways to their goals as the difficulty level increases is one of the key ways that students learn to overcome and strategize for themselves (Kiryakova et al., 2014).

Other Platforms

While I unabashedly evangelize for the use of Classcraft, it is not the only way to implement a gamified classroom. CourseSites, Moodle, Vula Sakai, A+, QizBox,

Diagnosys (specifically for math classes), Curatr, ClassDojo, and BadgeVille all show up in the research literature about gamification (Dicheva et al., 2015; Kiryakova et al., 2014; Turan et al., 2016). Instructors can also choose not to use any platform, and do things manually instead (Mitchell et al., 2013). Kahoot, Socrative, FlipQuiz, Ribbon Hero, and other apps or websites can also provide space for a limited game, say within one class period or for one quiz (Kiryakova et al., 2014; Turan et al., 2016) and are therefore not direct substitutes for a comprehensive system like Classcraft that is meant to cover the entire course.

Badges can be created through BadgeOS and BadgeStack on WordPress or through Mozilla's Open Badges Project (Kiryakova et al., 2014). Some schools may also pay for Credly from Pearson or other badge platforms; sometimes these are referred to as digital credential platforms. Keep in mind, however, that manually creating badges can be a time-consuming process. Getting them to integrate into a learning management system takes time and should be well-tested before using them in class.

Case Study: Human Sexuality Course

I had been using Classcraft (Premium) for three years at the time of this course in Fall 2022, in both lower-level Intro to Sociology classes and upper-level Sociology electives. There are no prerequisites for this sophomore-level class, and it draws in students from several different majors. For example, the university has the only gender and sexuality studies program left in the state of Oklahoma (other universities only have gender studies or women's studies programs, not the sexuality component), and many of these students filled the roster. Having almost thirty students in this class made this a little on the larger side.

As I considered whether to use Classcraft in this class, I was thinking about three major challenges using Classcraft would bring. First, even though this is a sociology course, most of the students are non-sociology majors. I have a bit of a reputation within my department for using nontraditional pedagogies like project-based learning and play-based pedagogy that require creativity instead of just discipline knowledge. While this is generally a good thing with students who have come to expect it of me, I did not expect non-majors would necessarily give me the same sort of grace. Our majors know me and know that there is truly a method to the madness of my strange pedagogical choices, and they know that it comes from a place of respect. I honestly thought that non-majors could revolt, or at least be less willing to go along with the game.

The second major challenge has to do with the lack of right and wrong answers. This is not entirely alien to me, as Sociology of Gender and even Intro to Sociology classes sometimes must balance opinions and facts and make room for several perspectives that often contradict each other. I was deeply concerned with how the Classcraft tools could work when there were better and worse answers, but no real "right answers." Several of the tools are designed with questions where there is a right and a wrong answer (i.e., you gain experience if you get the question right, you lose health if you get it wrong), so I worried that the Classcraft tools would be useless.

Thirdly, I was worried that the gamification would not work because of the sensitivity of the topics that we covered. So much of the Classcraft system relies on teamwork (and social-emotional learning), and I was concerned that a sociology class filled with non-sociology majors (many of whom do not know me) on a topic as politically and emotionally charged as sexuality could be a recipe for disaster. Note that the course began a few months after the June 2022 overturn of Roe v Wade, and in a very "red state" like Oklahoma, emotions were running high. Was it right of me to want to focus on building those "soft skills" when the topics we were dealing with in class were already feeling overwhelming and even traumatic for some students? Should I leave that extra SEL work to a class with an "easier" topic?

Even though I had these three challenges in my mind, I did have one important upside to using Classcraft in a sociology of sexuality course. I have seen repeatedly that gamification works so well in sociology because there truly is too much material for any one student, so you may as well let them pick what interests them. There was a sociological textbook that all students had to read, but our learning management system (D2L) was also filled with over 160 additional items that would be relegated to a recommended reading or watching list in a traditional class, and sadly never looked at by most students. Most of these additional pieces are news articles, TED Talks, other videos, and the like. I also had a list of about twenty books that students could use for old-school book reports if they chose.

Results

With these three challenges in mind, I still believed that Classcraft could work, and I felt comfortable taking the risk. I also had no plans to stop my play-based, tactile classroom activities, so I figured the Classcraft game would be the least of my worries. Play-based pedagogy is legitimate for adults as well as children, and making this clear to students that there is a purpose behind asking them to do something creative helps students who may not expect these fun activities in a college classroom. Have your brief defenses ready to explain why gamification and play work so well. It also helps to reiterate to students that you respect them, and you're coming from a caring place.

As for the concerns about no right and wrong answers, I avoided using some of the tools. We had no Boss Battles or Quests, and when I asked questions using the Wheel of Destiny random picker, I made clear when a question had several "correct" answers. Before I would take away a heart for a missed question, I would ask students to explain or justify their thinking. Often, a student would either realize their answer was indefensible and change their answer, or they would give a perfectly reasonable justification that I had not thought of, and I ended up counting their answer as correct. I should point out that the lack of Quests had as much to do with the non-linear nature of the topic as the lack of clear, correct answers. Instructors can create Quests where students only have to attempt an answer—not necessarily give the right answer—to proceed in the quest.

My concerns about the sensitivity of the topics were legitimate, and I often had to spend more time validating students' feelings in that class than in any other class I've ever taught. However, gamification did not seem to affect this. I suspect that I would have been doing more emotional work even if I had not used Classcraft. My concerns that it would be too much to focus on building soft skills when so many students are processing trauma in this class were misguided at best. I should have had more faith in the emotional intelligence of our students since so many of them have experienced very adult problems. I would have needed to use trauma-informed educational practices anyway, and this class is the one that really needs it. Giving students practice in having hard discussions is so important, I'm embarrassed that I once thought that I should avoid soft skills work in this class. This is the very class where those soft skills are most needed. If anything, being upfront with students that this class has a secondary focus on improving their soft skills gave me the freedom to ask questions like "Is there a more respectful way to talk about that," whenever students fell into disrespectful ways of talking. In a more traditional class, I probably would have had to call students out when they unknowingly used a disrespectful term, which would have been more awkward for everyone involved.

I should point out that on the first day, I talked at length about respecting everyone's life experiences and our activity had them decorating blank boxes with their genders and sexualities. I instructed them to put things inside the box that they might keep to themselves, things that are private. On the outsides of their boxes, they were instructed to put what they present to others, things that are public. This was a way to set up a language about privacy and respecting each other's privacy, as I encouraged them to use the euphemism "that's inside the box" if they ever felt like someone was asking too personal a question.

The Practicalities, or How I Used Classcraft in Human Sexuality

The class met twice a week for sixteen weeks, and students needed to get to level 30 by the end of the semester to receive full credit on the 80% of their grade that was Classcraft. (The remaining 20% of their grade came from participation in their Packback discussion board.) Students needed 750 XP for each level up, and I set hearts and crystals to regenerate one per day. I set up the Teams to try to give them as much (visible) diversity as possible, including making certain that each team had some Mages, Guardians, and Healers. No students remained Adventurers/Explorers.

The typical class period would start with me taking attendance using the Class Dashboard and giving all present students 200XP and 30 Gold for "Showing up to class on time and being ready to engage." Then we would have a "Riders of Vay" random event. I kept most of the pre-suggested random events but added some. Most of these events are good or neutral, but there are a few bad ones (e.g., a random person loses a heart) to keep students anticipating. I recommend adding a random event that calls for students to impersonate a luminary in your field. I also added a random event that called for a little extra XP given to anyone who emailed me a sociology meme, which I enjoyed as much as the students.

If students seemed motivated and I had the sense that they had been reading their textbooks, we skipped using the Wheel of Destiny to ask random students questions about the text. When we did use the Wheel of Destiny, I found it faster to have it pick teams instead of individual students, as I often did not have 25 questions to ask, and it seemed unfair to not give everyone a chance when we used it. I suspect that if we had used Wheel of Destiny every class period, I would not have been as concerned because everyone would have eventually had the chance; Classcraft does go through every student or team before restarting the random selection, even if several days have passed. Wheel of Destiny questions won students 75 XP and 10 Gold if they got it correct and lost them one heart if they missed it.

The bulk of our class time was spent "completing invited activities," which garnered students 150XP and 25 Gold each. Most 75-minute class periods involved at least a couple of activities, meaning that students who showed up to class and participated got about 500XP, just from showing up. Since 750XP was needed to level up, and students got used to the idea of needing to level up and come to class twice a week; they understood that they needed to do a few homework essays for each class. Turning in a reflection/reaction essay over a class reading (either from the textbook or on D2L) is the positive behavior I use whenever students read or watch something recommended on our learning management system and turn in a summary/reaction essay. It merited them 200XP and 30 Gold, the same as being on time to class. Extra Experience "Quickies" only netted them 100 XP and 15 gold each and were clearly marked in the learning management system. There actually weren't many of these, as they were very short new pieces or very short videos, and I would likely do away with this designation as most students still gave impressively thorough reaction essays, so I would often award students either "invited activity" (150XP) or the normal "reflection/reaction essay" (200XP) amounts.

"Contributing to the classroom community" won students 125XP and 20 Gold and was not used very often. It was typically used if I saw a student do something particularly kind for another student, or if a student asked an especially good question or made a very novel point in our discussions. Students could also win 150XP and 25 gold if their Packback post was featured, giving a Classcraft tie-in to remind students of the other component of their grade. A few posts were featured each week.

Besides missing a "Wheel of Destiny" question, the other ways students could lose hearts was by "choosing to be unkind to others" (loss of three hearts) or "choosing to disengage" (loss of two hearts). I almost never use these in any of my classes, as it is generally enough just to have them as a possibility to keep students from doing these behaviors, and I did not use them in Human Sexuality. Very few students even lost hearts from missing "Wheel of Destiny" questions, which led some students to say that they wished they had picked to be Mages instead of Guardians. In fairness, at least in my classes with how I focus on the positive behaviors almost exclusively, the benefit of the Guardians having the most hearts is not useful.

The ultimate grade distribution of the class was fairly uneven, with over half the class ending up with As. There were a handful of Bs and Cs from students who didn't quite make it to level 30 and a handful of failing students. This is sadly typical of my university and our student body, as so many of them are dealing with real-life problems, and simply stop attending classes and disengage with all their course material. It is notable that the COVID pandemic was still actively affecting students in the fall of 2022, even though many universities were adamant about getting back to normal.

Conclusion

Classcraft specifically gives students a sense of control over their grades, as well as a shared cultural language to talk about their grades. Younger and older students alike intuitively understand the ideas of health, experience, and avatars whether they identify with the gamer subculture or not. As with all gamification efforts, the more ways students can add points to their avatar, the more choices they have of work to do, and the better they can find assignments that they are motivated to complete. It helps students build those "soft skills" that are so desperately needed in our economy. Setting boundaries at the beginning of the course helped create the classroom as a safe space where students could talk candidly, which helped with discussions throughout the semester.

References

Abramovich, S., Schunn, C., & Higashi, R. M. (2013). Are badges useful in education?: It depends upon the type of badge and expertise of learner. *Educational Technology Research and Development, 61*(2), 217–232. https://d oi.org/10.1007/s11423-013-9289-2

Arnold, B. J. (2014). Gamification in education. *Proceedings of the American Society of Business and Behavioral Sciences, 21*(1), 32–39.

Bain, K. (2004). *What the best college teachers do.* Harvard University Press.

Bain, K. (2021). *Super courses: The future of teaching and learning.* Princeton University Press. https://press.princeton.edu/books/hardcover/9780691185 460/super-courses

Benson, B. K. (1997). Scaffolding (Coming to terms). *English Journal, 86*(7), 126–127.

Brookfield, S. D., & Preskill, S. (2012). *Discussion as a way of teaching: Tools and techniques for democratic classrooms.* John Wiley & Sons.

Bryman, A. (2004). *The Disneyization of society.* SAGE Publications Ltd. https:// www.goodreads.com/book/show/814958.The_Disneyization_of_Society

Buckley, P., & Doyle, E. (2016). Gamification and student motivation. *Interactive Learning Environments, 24*(6), 1162–1175. https://doi.org/10.1080/10494820 .2014.964263

Canada Economic Development for Quebec Regions. (2018, May 18). *Classcraft Studios: Its educational game will be available to teachers and students around the world* [News releases]. https://www.canada.ca/en/economic-development-quebec-regions/news/2018/05/classcraft-studios-its-educati onal-game-will-be-available-to-teachers-and-students-around-the-world.html

Caponetto, I., Earp, J., & Ott, M. (2014). Gamification and education: A literature review. *European Conference on Games Based Learning, 1*, 50.

Codish, D., & Ravid, G. (2014). Personality based gamification: Educational gamification for extroverts and introverts. *Proceedings of the 9th CHAIS Conference for the Study of Innovation and Learning Technologies: Learning in the Technological Era, 1*, 36–44. https://www.academia.edu/download/448 75703/Personality_Based_GamificationEducationa20160418-26859-5o7aql.pdf

Cook-Sather, A., Bovill, C., & Felten, P. (2014). *Engaging students as partners in learning and teaching: A guide for faculty* (1st ed.). Jossey-Bass.

Deterding, S., Dixon, D., Khaled, R., & Nacke, L. (2011). From game design elements to gamefulness: Defining "gamification." *Proceedings of the 15th International Academic MindTrek Conference: Envisioning Future Media Environments*, 9–15. https://doi.org/10.1145/2181037.2181040

Devers, C. J., & Gurung, R. A. R. (2015). Critical perspective on gamification in education. In T. Reiners & L. C. Wood (Eds.), *Gamification in Education and Business* (pp. 417–430). Springer International Publishing. https://doi.org/10. 1007/978-3-319-10208-5_21

Dicheva, D., & Dichev, C. (2015). Gamification in education: Where are we in 2015? *E-Learn: World Conference on E-Learning in Corporate, Government, Healthcare, and Higher Education*, 1445–1454.

Dicheva, D., Dichev, C., Agre, G., & Angelova, G. (2015). Gamification in education: A systematic mapping study. *Journal of Educational Technology & Society, 18*(3), 75–88.

Durlak, J., Weissberg, R. P., Dymnicki, A., Taylor, R., & Schellinger, K. (2011). The impact of enhancing students' social and emotional learning: A meta-analysis of school-based universal interventions. *Child Development, 82*(1), 405–432. https://doi.org/10.1111/j.1467-8624.2010.01564.x

Dweck, C. S. (2007). *Mindset: The new psychology of success.* Ballantine Books.

Erenli, K. (2013). The impact of gamification-recommending education scenarios. *International Journal of Emerging Technologies in Learning (IJET), 8*(2013).

Forbes Coaches Council. (2019, January 22). *Council post: 15 soft skills you need to succeed when entering the workforce.* Forbes. https://www.forbes.com/site s/forbescoachescouncil/2019/01/22/15-soft-skills-you-need-to-succeed-whe n-entering-the-workforce/

Fotaris, P., Mastoras, T., Leinfellner, R., & Rosunally, Y. (2016). Climbing up the leaderboard: An empirical study of applying gamification techniques to a computer programming class. *Electronic Journal of E-Learning, 14*(2), 94–110.

Freitas, S. A. A., Lacerda, A. R., Calado, P. M., Lima, T. S., & Canedo, E. D. (2017). Gamification in education: A methodology to identify student's profile. *2017 IEEE Frontiers in Education Conference (FIE)*, 1–8.

Furdu, I., Tomozei, C., & Kose, U. (2017). *Pros and cons gamification and gaming in classroom* (arXiv:1708.09337). arXiv. http://arxiv.org/abs/1708.09337

Hallifax, S., Serna, A., Marty, J.-C., & Lavoué, É. (2019). Adaptive gamification in education: A literature review of current trends and developments. *Transforming Learning with Meaningful Technologies: 14th European Conference on Technology Enhanced Learning, EC-TEL 2019, Delft, The Netherlands, September 16–19, 2019, Proceedings 14*, 294–307.

Hanstedt, P. (2018). *Creating wicked students: Designing courses for a complex world.* Stylus Publishing LLC.

Huang, B., & Hew, K. F. (2015). Do points, badges and leaderboard increase learning and activity: A quasi-experiment on the effects of gamification. *Proceedings of the 23rd International Conference on Computers in Education,* 275–280. https://www.researchgate.net/profile/Khe-Hew/publication/28600 1811_Do_points_badges_and_leaderboard_increase_learning_and_activity_ A_quasi-experiment_on_the_effects_of_gamification/links/5665404708ae15 e746333d22/Do-points-badges-and-leaderboard-increase-learning-and-acti vity-A-quasi-experiment-on-the-effects-of-gamification.pdf

Huang, W. H.-Y., & Soman, D. (2013). Gamification of education. *Report Series: Behavioural Economics in Action, 29*(4), 37.

Kim, B. (2015). Gamification in education and libraries. *Library Technology Reports, 51*(2), 20–28.

Kiryakova, G., Angelova, N., & Yordanova, L. (2014). Gamification in education. *Proceedings of 9th International Balkan Education and Science Conference, 1,* 679–684.

Majuri, J., Koivisto, J., & Hamari, J. (2018). Gamification of education and learning: A review of empirical literature. *Proceedings of the 2nd International GamiFIN Conference, GamiFIN 2018.*

Manzano-León, A., Camacho-Lazarraga, P., Guerrero, M. A., Guerrero-Puerta, L., Aguilar-Parra, J. M., Trigueros, R., & Alias, A. (2021). Between level up and game over: A systematic literature review of gamification in education. *Sustainability, 13*(4), 2247.

Martí-Parreño, J., Méndez-Ibáñez, E., & Alonso-Arroyo, A. (2016). The use of gamification in education: A bibliometric and text mining analysis. *Journal of Computer Assisted Learning, 32*(6), 663–676.

Medica Ružić, I., & Dumančić, M. (2015). Gamification in education. *Informatologia, 48*(3–4), 198–204.

Miller, C. (2013). The gamification of education. *Developments in Business Simulation and Experiential Learning: Proceedings of the Annual ABSEL Conference, 40.*

Mitchell, N., Danino, N., & May, L. (2013). Motivation and manipulation: A gamification approach to influencing undergraduate attitudes in computing. *7th European Conference on Games Based Learning, ECGBL 2013, 1,* 394–400.

Nah, F. F.-H., Telaprolu, V. R., Rallapalli, S., & Venkata, P. R. (2013). Gamification of education using computer games. *Human Interface and the Management of Information. Information and Interaction for Learning, Culture, Collaboration and Business, 15th International Conference, HCI International 2013, Las Vegas, NV, USA, July 21-26, 2013, Proceedings, Part III 15,* 99–107.

Nah, F. F.-H., Zeng, Q., Telaprolu, V. R., Ayyappa, A. P., & Eschenbrenner, B. (2014). Gamification of education: A review of literature. *HCI in Business: First International Conference, HCIB 2014, Held as Part of HCI International 2014, Heraklion, Crete, Greece, June 22-27, 2014. Proceedings 1,* 401–409.

Nicholson, S. (2013). *Exploring gamification techniques for classroom management.* Games+Learning+Society 9.0, Madison WI. http://scottnichols on.com/pubs/gamificationtechniquesclassroom.pdf

Ofosu-Ampong, K. (2020). The shift to gamification in education: A review on dominant issues. *Journal of Educational Technology Systems, 49*(1), 113–137.

Oliveira, W., Hamari, J., Shi, L., Toda, A. M., Rodrigues, L., Palomino, P. T., & Isotani, S. (2023). Tailored gamification in education: A literature review and future agenda. *Education and Information Technologies, 28*(1), 373–406.

Ortiz-Rojas, M., Chiluiza, K., & Valcke, M. (2019). Gamification through leaderboards: An empirical study in engineering education. *Computer Applications in Engineering Education, 27*(4), 777–788. https://doi.org/10.10 02/cae.12116

Prensky, M. (2001). Digital natives, digital immigrants part 2: Do they really think differently? *On the Horizon, 9*(6), 1–6. https://doi.org/10.1108/1074812 0110424843

Rabah, J., Cassidy, R., & Beauchemin, R. (2018). Gamification in education: Real benefits or edutainment. *17th European Conference on E-Learning, Athens, Greece,* 489–497.

Rockwood, K. (2021, May 28). *The hard facts about soft skills.* SHRM. https://www.shrm.org/hr-today/news/hr-magazine/summer2021/pages/why-soft-skills-are-important.aspx

Sandusky, S. L. (2015). Gamification in education. *Education, Computer Science.* https://www.semanticscholar.org/paper/Gamification-in-Education-Sandusky/26dd514378802e611fa496cb68d3bd262181df1c

Sheldon, L. (2020). *The multiplayer classroom: Designing coursework as a game.* CRC Press. https://www.routledge.com/The-Multiplayer-Classroom-Designing-Coursework-as-a-Game/Sheldon/p/book/9780367249052

Stott, A., & Neustaedter, C. (2013). *Analysis of gamification in education* (p. 36). School of Interactive Arts and Technology, Simon Fraser University.

Surendeleg, G., Murwa, V., Yun, H.-K., & Kim, Y. S. (2014). The role of gamification in education–a literature review. *Contemporary Engineering Sciences, 7*(29), 1609–1616.

Swacha, J. (2021). State of research on gamification in education: A bibliometric survey. *Education Sciences, 11*(2), 69.

Toda, A. M., Valle, P. H., & Isotani, S. (2018). The dark side of gamification: An overview of negative effects of gamification in education. *Higher Education for All. From Challenges to Novel Technology-Enhanced Solutions: First International Workshop on Social, Semantic, Adaptive and Gamification Techniques and Technologies for Distance Learning, HEFA 2017, Maceió, Brazil, March 20–24, 2017, Revised Selected Papers 1,* 143–156.

Turan, Z., Avinc, Z., Kara, K., & Goktas, Y. (2016). Gamification and education: Achievements, cognitive loads, and views of students. *Int. J. Emerg. Technol. Learn., 11*(7), 64–69.

US Bureau of Labor Statistics. (2021, August 31). *Number of jobs, labor market experience, marital status, and health: Results from a national longitudinal survey summary* [News Release]. Number of Jobs, Labor Market Experience, Marital Status, and Health. https://www.bls.gov/news.release/nlsoy.nr0.htm

Van Roy, R., & Zaman, B. (2018). Need-supporting gamification in education: An assessment of motivational effects over time. *Computers & Education, 127,* 283–297

Young, S. (2023, May 11). *HMH acquires Canadian EdTech company Classcraft—Classcraft Blog.* Resource Hub for Schools and Districts. https://www.classcraft.com/resources/blog/hmh-acquires-canadian-edtech-company-classcraft/

List of Contributors

Andrea Trudeau. She is a PhD candidate in Instructional Technology at Northern Illinois University and a library information specialist with 26 years of K-12 teaching experience in a public middle school setting. Throughout her career, she has taken a student-centered approach while embracing innovative teaching practices and technology tools to engage and empower her students. In turn, this inspired her to research the effects of cinematic virtual reality on the empathic responses of adolescent students. Learn more at noshhlibrarian.com

Jonathan Simmons. Postdoc researcher at the University of Connecticut. He holds a PhD in Curriculum and Instruction and has been an elementary school teacher in the United States and internationally. His research explores innovative instructional approaches and the development of intercultural competence in pre-service teachers.

Jess Wythe. Early Career Researcher and Lecturer for the Department of Childhood Youth and Community at Birmingham City University in the United Kingdom. She has research interests in gaming, educational school trips, and creative and innovative pedagogical interventions for children with autistic spectrum disorders. Jess is currently researching the learning and educational benefits of school trips to heritage sites for children and young people with special educational needs for her doctorate thesis, with ambitions of contributing towards making learning more engaging and accessible for all.

Anastasia R. Wickham. She began her career as an educator by teaching secondary English, Spanish, and ELL classes, as well as working as a reading specialist. This experience, combined with a Ph.D. in Instructional Leadership and Academic Curriculum and over a decade in higher education, informs her current work in supporting pre-service teachers in underserved urban and rural communities. Currently, Dr. Wickham focuses on providing an accessible, affordable pathway to a job-embedded teaching degree through her work at Reach University, where she serves as a member of the faculty and an administrator.

Jeaneen S. Miller Canfield. Visiting Assistant Professor of English at the University of Central Oklahoma. Her scholarship has appeared in Praxis: A Writing Center Journal, Composition Forum (forthcoming Fall 2024), a book chapter in Teaching Critical Reading and Writing in the Era of Fake News, and she has presented her work at various conferences. Her research interests include the intersections of cartography and writing pedagogy, visual rhetoric, multimodal composition, digital literacies (including AI tools), and critical pedagogy. She also is deeply committed to helping students gain their own voice and learn to publish their works. Currently, she is co-authoring two works with former students. One project is about students' use of AI writing bots (chiefly ChatGPT), and the other is about her journey, as well as a student's insightful perspective, regarding accessibility for visually impaired students.

Lia Schuermann. She is a mixed Chicana PhD candidate at Texas Woman's University (TWU)'s Rhetoric program. She is a Graduate Teaching Assistant (Lead Instructor) teaching in TWU's First-Year Composition (FYC) program. Her teaching focuses on how digital and multimodal composition can create alternative spaces for students to collaborate and build community. She's presented at the Popular/American Culture Association (PCA) and Computers & Writing conferences in 2023 on how digital games and game design can be part of FYC and writing courses.

Dr. Laura Dumin. She obtained her PhD in English from Oklahoma State University in 2010. She is a professor of English and Technical Writing at the University of Central Oklahoma. Laura has been experimenting with transformative learning (TL) tools and scholarship of teaching and learning methods (SoTL) in the classroom for over 7 years. She finds that when students are engaged in the lessons, learning can happen organically, leading to more interesting class periods and longer-term gains in understanding concepts. Laura mixes her background in technical writing into all her courses, bringing ideas of audience and clear communication into assignments.

When she is not teaching, she works as a co-managing editor for the *Journal of Transformative Learning*. Laura was a campus SoTL mentor, directs the Technical Writing BA, and advises the Composition and Rhetoric MA program. She has also been exploring the impact of AI and large language models on writing classrooms and runs a Facebook learning community to allow instructors to learn from each other. https://www.facebook.com/groups/632930835501841

Daniel Atwood. Doctoral student in musicology at Northwestern University and a guitar instructor at Three Rivers College. His dissertation explores early modern English popular music culture, and his research interests also include video game music and ethnographies of musical experiences in everyday life. He has presented his research at the conferences of the Society for Seventeenth-Century Music, the Association Répertoire International d'Iconographie Musicale, the Royal Music Association, the Symposium on Medieval and Renaissance Studies, and the Popular Culture Association.

Leeda Copley. A lifelong gamer who also happens to hold a PhD in Ageing Studies. She works as an associate professor for the University of Central Oklahoma, so she has enough money to buy new games and have a home to store all her gaming consoles. She teaches sociology and gerontology courses and does research that focuses on the intersections between gender and pop culture.

Index